Great Beginnings

CEL Series
Conference on English Leadership

The Conference on English Leadership, an organization within the National Council of Teachers of English, is composed of English department leaders and other English educators who hold a common interest in English program development and teacher training. Through this series, CEL encourages discussion of critical issues in the professional development of English department chairs, English/language arts curriculum supervisors, and others having supervisory roles in the areas of English/language arts education from elementary through secondary levels.

1998 CEL Executive Committee

Great Beginnings

Reflections and Advice for New English Language Arts Teachers and the People Who Mentor Them

Edited by

Ira Hayes
Syosset High School
Syosset, New York

Conference on English Leadership

National Council of Teachers of English
1111 W. Kenyon Road, Urbana, Illinois 61801-1096

Cover Design and Prepress Services: City Desktop Productions, Inc.

Interior Design: Doug Burnett

NCTE Stock Number: 18887-3050

It is the policy of NCTE in its journals and other publications to provide a forum for the open discussion of ideas concerning the content and the teaching of English and the language arts. Publicity accorded to any particular point of view does not imply endorsement by the Executive Committee, the Board of Directors, or the membership at large, except in announcements of policy, where such endorsement is clearly specified.

Library of Congress Cataloging-in-Publication Data

Great beginnings : reflections and advice for new English language arts teachers and the people who mentor them / edited by Ira Hayes.
    p.   cm.
   "Conference on English Leadership."
   "NCTE stock number: 18887-3050"–T.p. verso
   ISBN 0-8141-1888-7
    1. English teachers—Training of—United States. 2. Language arts teachers—Training of—United States. 3. English language—Study and teaching—United States. 4. Mentoring in education. I. Hayes, Ira. II. Conference on English Leadership.
PE1068.U5G69 1998
428'.0071'173—dc21   98-20699
                                                                          CIP

Contents

Acknowledgments

The editor wishes to express his gratitude to the following: the CEL Executive Committee for encouraging and supporting the project; the other members of the CEL monograph committee, Jeff Golub and Barbara Thompson, who served in the chapter selection process; the NCTE review committee, June Langford Berkeley and Louann Reid, who read the articles in the existing monograph; and the authors of the chapters in the monograph for their passion and expertise.

Introduction

Ira Hayes
Syosset High School, Syosset, New York

What are the essentials for a great beginning in English education? In our first CEL volume, we address this question and other related ones. What support do talented new teachers need? How can experienced educators best help them? How can supervisors of English education balance support with evaluation? What are exemplary programs for new teachers? Who and what have been the stimuli for the "great beginnings" of experienced English educators? Our call for manuscripts invited educators at all levels to address these issues. We invited beginning teachers to reflect on their first years and experienced teachers to speak about both exemplary programs and their own beginnings, great or otherwise.

In reading the manuscripts, I was reminded of my own beginnings as an English teacher in a large New York City public high school. Earning an M.A. in August, I began teaching in September. I observed a lot of highly literate teachers talking about books and students. "It's OK to be like them," I thought. But I cannot remember the English chair or any other teacher, experienced or otherwise, offering me one suggestion about my four remedial classes and one regular class. My only real guidance was trial and error. I learned immediately not to write out a disciplinary referral in front of a student; I realized that if I wanted to remain coherent, I could not teach an inane story such as "Are They Baboons or Blaboons?" four times in one day. I did have energy and enjoyed standing up and carrying on in front of a roomful of students who listened to me. The next year, I taught at another Brooklyn high school, Midwood High School, my professional home for the next twenty years. In my first years there, I received superb training in the craft of teaching from two sources: a superb English chair and a group of young teachers. The English chair was an "old-line" supervisor, Sol Schlakman. His first name was "Mister"; I remember only one person calling him "Sol." He nurtured not through "warm fuzzies" but through his aura of expertise. He communicated his love of literature and the craft of teaching. I still believe what he taught me about the ingredients of a fine lesson. And in my first few years at the school, I met a group of colleagues, all starting out, all eager, all teaching for the love of it, none of us suffering fools gladly. From one another we learned how to teach and how to live. It was a charmed circle; the charm lasted for many years.

Sol Schlakman retired; Sylvia Rosman, a teacher I did not know well, became chair. I became her assistant. In the five years we worked together, she became my most important mentor, both as a teacher and a future English department chair. She was a great mentor for many reasons. First, she made me feel good; she regularly told me that what I was doing was excellent. She also let me in on the process of what she thought was good teaching and supervising. She never led by confrontation. She knew that most people want to do a good job, that it was important to realize that we would live with these people for a long time. And she loved what she was doing. An intellectual with a razor-sharp wit, she could think of no more important and joyous a professional life than to be involved in education at Midwood High School. She was a great role model. I think of her often, her combination of emotional and intellectual support.

In preparing this volume, I was struck by how often the writers mention the emotional ingredient as well as pedagogical strategies. They talk about the need for programs that encourage sharing and mentoring, of balancing the best in student-centered pedagogy with the need to establish authority. As a result of reading all the manuscripts, I have helped beginning teachers in new ways. I can now ask a new teacher, "How can I best help you?" I can say, "Just keep doing what you're doing; I can give you the freedom to try whatever you think might work. Don't worry about succeeding all the time."

This volume is a combination of memoirs and suggestions for new teachers and for English leaders. The first selections are memoirs. In her extended, inspiring essay, Gayle Bolt Price says, "All things considered, there is no finer way to spend a life." Susan Joan Fishbein remembers her twelfth-grade English teacher, who later became her mentor and first supervisor. Maureen Neal advises new teachers, "Don't take yourself too seriously." Kenneth Simons writes about becoming a new teacher at forty, comparing his expectations with reality. Donald M. Shafer's essay is about his career as both an English teacher and a department chair. Diana Wagner Marmaluk recalls her first years teaching in a small school, reminding us to share our successes and fears. Wang Zhijun's memoir is about her career teaching English in China. Finally, Julia M. Emig reflects on the difficulties and pleasures of her first year teaching in a rough Boston-area high school. In looking back, each author mentions both an important person and a sustaining vision.

The next chapters speak to new teachers. Some selections speak variously about a philosophic framework; others talk of specific concerns; and still others give practical suggestions. The first articles focus on the personal and emotional in teaching, something that the young teachers were not prepared to deal with. F. Todd Goodson writes of the complex process of new teachers fitting in to the existing teacher culture of a particular school. Mary C. McMackin and Judith A. Boccia examine problems in teacher retention and a program designed to combat high attrition rates. Regina Paxton Foehr writes of ways for new teachers to avoid burn-out. Paul Heilker remembers his own beginnings. He says, "What I was thoroughly unprepared for was just how personal and emotional teaching is. And this personal, emotional reality is . . . the single most important thing a beginning teacher should know." The next articles are full of practical suggestions. In their respective essays, Brenda L. Dyer and Janet Gebhart Auten address important issues of how new teachers can practice the best in student-centered pedagogy and establish themselves as authority figures at the same time, while Sean Meehan talks of establishing a productive writing/reading workshop. In a memoir whose reflections give support to new teachers, Inga Harmon Smith talks about Project BOOST. Then Mary Theresa Kyne writes of the characteristics of effective educational leaders and effective teachers. Finally, the essays by Richard F. Gaspar and Gerald Mackey provide lots of specific *do's* and *don'ts*, suggestions with lots of common sense.

The extensive "For the English Leader" chapters present leaders with specific guidelines, programs, and strategies for developing new teachers. Lists are boring, but some striking contributors, with a summary of their articles, belong on one. Jane E. Harvey, Daniel A. Heller, Jennifer S. McConnell, and Debra J. Williams share their staff development program. Thomas Philion provides supervisors with strategies for becoming less authoritative. Lisa Birnbaum focuses on the weight of supervisory language. Sheryl Rubin reflects on the changes in her observational techniques brought about by our changing pedagogy. Charlotte Adomaitis gives practical suggestions for creating workshops for new teachers, while Susan A. Wasserman mentions specific support programs for them. Noreen

Duffy Copeland talks of new teachers keeping journals. And John Zubizarreta focuses on the teaching portfolio.

What this volume reinforces is how passionate and committed the best teachers are—yet teaching is a craft that can be practiced and learned. The most important ingredient for a great beginning as a teacher is liking those whom you teach. If you don't like them, you have no business in the classroom. Learning the craft comes next; it is a skill than cannot be left to chance. This volume demonstrates the passion and the techniques that lead to excellence. I hope much of it resonates with you.

I Memoirs

Knowing the importance of stories to our understanding of where we've been and where we're going, the eight experienced educators here describe their "great beginnings" in the classroom. From the 1950s to the 1990s, and from rural communities to inner-city schools, these teachers recall the surprises, the challenges, and the joys they found in setting out on their journeys as teachers. Although each experience is unique, common themes recur: the sometimes discouraging, sometimes exciting difference between careful plans and chaotic realities; the importance of supportive mentors and colleagues in finding our own way; and, above all, the recognition that we learn at least as much as we teach in our interactions with those most important fellow travelers, our students.

1 An Experienced Teacher Looks Back

Gayle Bolt Price
Gardner-Webb University

Gayle Bolt Price finds, in looking back over a long career in teaching, that what remains most vivid in her memory is not lesson plans or theories, but the unique individuals she has taught. For all of them, be they young or old, skilled or struggling, her "only really significant lesson" has been, "You can do it!"

During the past twenty years, I have attempted to teach some aspect of English to the following student populations: (1) in an inner-city high school, to nonreaders and functional illiterates, as well as student journalists, honors juniors, and college-bound seniors who sometimes slept in class because they went home after seventh period to take care of babies or to sell drugs or to work at night as short-order cooks and textile-mill doffers (to help their mothers buy groceries); (2) in a solid suburban high school, to student journalists and college-bound juniors and honors seniors as well as kids who also slept in class because they worked third shift somewhere (often to pay for the turbo-charged Camaros in the school parking lot); and (3) in public and private two-year colleges, private liberal arts colleges, and large state universities, to countless freshmen—some decidedly unprepared, some the prizes of their respective high schools, some traditional college-aged youths with no responsibilities and some middle-aged adults with families—struggling to learn to write acceptably "academic" prose as well as to "do college." In all, they have presented a dizzying array of students of all races and many cultures, learning the truths to be gleaned from literature, even when much of it seemed far removed from their lives. There have been poor readers trying to gain enough eleventh-hour proficiency from college reading improvement courses to handle hundreds of pages of assigned reading in freshman history and biology texts. There have also been Africans and Arabs and Asians, Brazilians and Pakistanis and Russians (almost without exception highly motivated and extraordinarily conscientious) polishing their English in order to excel in an American university. Outside the traditional classroom, I have also taught (4) in a summer cultural exchange program, to thirty-five Japanese teenage boys cramming in enough conversational English to carry them through a month's tour of the United States and then take them back to their private Tokyo high school to impress family and friends. And (5) in a county Mental Health Adult Day Treatment Center, to barely literate adults painfully reaching out to make contact with the "real" world, their task made *almost* impossible because of their minds being numbed by drugs to control their schizophrenia or because of the years spent in state mental hospitals.

My teaching experiences have been most notable, perhaps, for their diversity. But I did not dream of or prepare for that diversity when I was a young teacher-in-training. I did not prepare for it because nothing about my small-segregated-Southern-town-conservative-middle-class upbringing had given me a hint of what I would face. Thus the shape my career has taken is nothing like the dream of it that I had when starting out: a dream of standing before interested students who were similar to myself in background, motivation, and ability, and of teaching in ways similar to the best ways that I had been taught. And curiously, when I look back on my twenty years of standing in classrooms as "The Teacher," I can barely see the classrooms or the classes at all, and except for maybe those of the past five years, I don't remember the substance of a single "lesson" I have taught. Flooding my memory, however, are images of individual students who, for no discernible reason, stand out from the masses that they comprised. These individuals have little in common that I can readily see, except that they have taught me far more than I ever taught them. From them I have learned some essential truths about teaching that could help new teachers make a better beginning than I made. Nothing can smooth the waters completely; teaching is hard work because it involves shaping the most complex of raw materials, human beings. And after all, there is much value in life from swimming hard through rough water. Nevertheless, knowing fully those essential truths at the outset would have given me a faster and smoother leap from the starting block, with fewer student casualties in my wake during the early years. Since those truths have come to me through those individuals, I would like to share a few of their stories.

Michael

Michael was a sixteen-year-old ninth grader who slept in class and would not turn in any work at all; he was the first to show me how poorly my dream matched reality. During the first two weeks of my teaching career, I exhausted my entire repertoire of punishments trying to get him both to stay awake and to perform. One day I sat down to talk with him while his classmates were working on a composition. Delighted at the attention, he grinned, showing straight, white teeth punctuated by one gleaming gold incisor.

"Why don't you stay awake in class?" I asked.

"'Cause I work at night, and school is the only time I have to sleep," he answered pleasantly.

"Why don't you quit your job?" I asked.

"'Cause my Mama need the money," he beamed.

"Why don't you at least do your classwork?" I asked weakly.

"'Cause I don't know how to do all this writin' you always askin' us to do," he replied amiably.

"Oh, come on now, Michael, you can write about anything you want to," I cajoled. "You can do it; I know you can!"

Scratching his head doubtfully, he picked up his pencil. After twenty minutes I collected the first piece of work he had completed in two months of school. Again grinning broadly, he watched me out of the corner of his eye while I read this laboriously printed composition: "i im a cook in i cook eggs."

Two weeks later, on his seventeenth birthday (the legal age for ending compulsory education in our state), he dropped out of school, happy that now he could cook eggs at night and spend his days sleeping comfortably in his own bed. That was but one of many times when I have gone wearily home from school to write my letter of resignation, convinced my choice of career was a tragic mistake.

Benny Ray

In my second year of teaching I was a bit wiser about the abilities, or lack of them, of my charges, so after only a few days I discovered that Benny Ray, a perpetually silent ninth grader, could not read at all. Frustrated the previous year by trying to teach literary works from the canon to students like Michael, I had volunteered to take over the high school's remedial reading classes. The advantage of the move was that I had twenty, rather than thirty, students those periods and could spend a little more time one-on-one. The disadvantage was that I didn't have many materials that students even more proficient than Benny Ray could read. So I often had them write their own "stories," which I would then type up for them to read to each other. Benny Ray couldn't write anything except his name, but for several weeks I coaxed him to tell me a story that I could write down and that he could try to read back to me. He responded each time by ducking inside the collar of the big sports-logo jacket and cap he always wore, and staring out at me with black, expressionless eyes.

One day I decided not to give up until I had pulled him out of his shell. I sat down beside him and for probably fifteen minutes suggested things he might "write" about. Finally deciding that I wasn't going away unless he said something, he started, at my suggestion, to tell me where he had gotten the big jacket and cap he always wore: He had hustled them from an older kid in his neighborhood during a game of "Horse" played at the basketball goal in the community park. Apparently this slight, silent boy had been something of a legend in his parts ever since. I printed it all out largely and neatly and then asked him to read it to me. He looked at me doubtfully, but haltingly began, and discovering that he could read all but a couple of words without help, he picked up speed, beginning to register the closest thing to excitement he ever exhibited. When the bell rang, he packed up his "story" and set off to his next class: resource.

Fifteen minutes later he appeared at my door, waving a note and flashing something I had never seen—a smile on his face. The note was from his resource teacher, delightedly telling me that Benny Ray had brought his "story" to class and read it to her without missing a word. It was, she said, the only thing she had ever seen him read. When I left that school two years later, Benny Ray still scored as a nonreader on standardized reading tests, but he could read his favorite magazine, *Sports Illustrated*.

Minnie

Minnie was a gray-haired, fifty-seven-year-old schizophrenic who had spent close to forty years—all of her adult life—in a state mental hospital, until the authorities had decided to purge the institutions of nonviolent psychotics whose illnesses could be controlled through medication, placing them in community-care settings. She spent her days in an Adult Mental Health Day Treatment Center, where I worked as a part-time teacher while pursuing graduate studies at a nearby university. My assignment was to develop individualized educational plans for each of the center's clients. Their needs ranged from reintroducing them to the good books they had enjoyed in their pre-illness days so that they could fill idle time with mentally stimulating activity, to preparing them to pass the GED exam so that they could hope to find gainful employment if their improvement continued, to— in the case of Minnie—attempting to make a small connection between an atrophied brain and the world that had been going on without her for nearly four decades.

From the beginning I was drawn by Minnie's sweet spirit and an air about her—she perpetually smiled but never spoke or laughed aloud—that suggested she was witness to some delightful secret world that I could hope to be invited into only if I proved myself worthy. I wanted to prove myself worthy. I spent as much as I could of my twice-weekly visits to the center with Minnie, teaching her the long forgotten mysteries of how to write and read her name and simple sentences about herself, as well as to add and to subtract. Over and over and over I would have her copy the words I had printed out for her and would gently prod her to read them back to me. Over and over and over she would count out simple sums by tapping her soft, bony fingers on the table. She would beam soundlessly when she got them right. By my next visit, she would have forgotten everything we had done before, and patiently we would begin again.

After several months of this, I was starting to feel, to say the least, discouraged. Then one day, without warning, a light seemed to go off in her strange, distant eyes (a deep brown surrounded by pale blue a little lighter than robins' eggs). I pulled out the writing she had copied the week before, a short paragraph of facts about her, and asked her to read it. She did it! She looked at me wonderingly and smiled broadly like a child who had just seen the real Santa Claus. I pulled out the math problems we had worked on for months, and she did them! For the first time, Minnie laughed out loud.

Robert

Robert was—is—the most brilliant person I have ever known. When I met him, he was a tall and gawky ninth grader with the obligatory pimples, assigned to my homeroom. He had never made anything less than an "A" in school—as his mother proudly told me at the PTA open house—and he had always shown equal aptitude in courses as diverse as English and math. He blushed and lowered his head, muttering "Aw, Mom" through an embarrassed grin. I did not teach him until two years later, when he appeared, to my delight, in my junior honors English class, and it was not for several months that I discovered he had astonishingly creative gifts as well.

But the shy innocence of his early adolescence had changed into a taciturn sullenness during the two years since he had been in my homeroom. I suspected it was the result of too much loneliness; he clearly had no peers. His classmates had long ago recognized his genius, and they therefore treated him with awed deference; there was no camaraderie with him, none of the teasing and joking and teenage banter that marked most of the rest of the class as the in-crowd of the high school. He responded with a casual aloofness clearly intended to signify that he did not care, but I watched and ached with unfulfilled longing to see the shy smile of two years before. At first his work for me was the brilliant stuff I had expected. I praised him profusely and often read his compositions and answers to essay exam questions to the class as models of perfection. He would come visit me after school, and we would talk about books and writers, conversations on a level I hadn't enjoyed since graduate school and had never expected to have again outside a college community. After awhile he cautiously began to show me his poetry and his drawings and to tell me about his musical compositions (he had had no formal musical training but listened avidly to classical music on public radio). I was astonished at the breadth of his accomplishments; his poetry, especially, was remarkable. I shuddered at my own inadequacy in being the one he seemed to have selected as mentor. My uneasiness turned to consternation when I started hearing reports from other teachers that he had quit doing their assignments, and I lay awake at night worrying about how to respond were the same thing to happen in my class—which, after a time, it did. Putting him on an independent study got him to the end of the year with his "A" average intact in English, but his grades plummeted in other subjects. My attempts to talk to him about his diminishing performance and the tragic waste of his enormous potential (he had, until that time, seemed to share his mother's dream of his winning a scholarship to a prestigious university, becoming the only person in their blue-collar family to go to college) resulted in fewer after-school visits and periods of uncomfortable silence when he did stop by. By the end of the year, when he came to turn in his final independent-study project, he said little when I told him I would be at a different school the next year but hoped he would stay in touch and let me know how his senior year went.

I did not hear from him again until the end of the following school year. I looked up from grading a stack of final exams to see him standing at my classroom door. He had walked the fifteen miles from his home to my school to tell me that he had dropped out of school two weeks before graduation, to protest the travesty he believed a high school diploma to be. Fighting back tears, I asked him what he intended to do next. He shrugged and said, "Travel."

I either heard from or saw him sporadically over the next sixteen years. He did travel some, and he continued to write poetry, although apparently no one ever saw it. Eventually he settled back in his hometown (I had left and did not return for eight years), and after a time he earned his GED. He worked at various low-paying jobs, seeming to like most his stint as a teacher's aide in a special school at a children's psychiatric hospital, but stayed longest as a clerk in a bicycle shop. He married a woman with a master's degree in school counseling. Eventually I was delighted to run into him and learn that he was about to graduate from the local community college, and as a result of his outstanding performance there, he had won a full scholarship to a prestigious private liberal arts university in our town. I have never been more pleased by any news. I was not surprised a couple of years later when he called to tell me that his performance at the university had just won him a fellowship from a national foundation to earn a Ph.D.—in English literature. He thanked me for "talking straight" to him, and for continuing to care about and believe in him for so many years. This time, I cried freely.

Paula

That Paula was Miss All-American-Best-All-Around-Teenager was clear to me from the first moment she bounced into my classroom to introduce herself at the high school where I was a new teacher and she was The-Student-in-Charge. To this day—and that was seventeen years ago—I do not know why she made me her pet teacher, but I have remained ever grateful. Not only could I always count on her to make me feel like a brilliant teacher with her performance in my senior honors English class, she also continually bailed me out as school newspaper advisor by spending hours after school to finish well the work of a lazy editor. Then she polished off the year by winning the school's Writing Achievement Award, being selected by the English faculty over very talented students in other classes, once again making me seem a superlative teacher when I had done absolutely nothing except place her in competition. Over the years there have been many students to whom I have taught nothing—because they were so bright and motivated that they taught themselves more effectively than I could ever hope to—but to no other have I taught nothing quite so brilliantly!

And I have been only one of many standing on the sidelines of Paula's adult life cheering her on, totally unsurprised that she has gone on to graduate from college with honors, serve as a missionary teacher in Jordan, travel the world, earn one graduate degree and begin another, and advance steadily in positions of responsibility and service to humankind. Many times I have wondered over her love for me, which has continued over the years, and many times an unexpected long-distance telephone call or note from Paula has lifted me out of despondency over some difficulty of my middle age. Just recently I was experiencing a prolonged one of those periods and had once again decided that I had made a tragic mistake in my choice of career, that I had wasted the twenty years I had spent thinking I was a teacher. At my lowest point, I received a letter from Paula, part of which read as follows:

> I'm years older and miles away from the classroom where you gave of yourself, as well as of what you knew about high school English. Yet, you and that year are close in my heart always. . . . As that 12th grade year wore on, I purposed in my heart to be just like you. I wanted to be a teacher. . . .
>
> Perhaps that's why I'm so reflective now. Last fall when I returned to Jordan to visit, I located several of my former students. It was wonderful to see what has become of them! Four of them are English teachers—your "granddaughters" in the field! Three are medical doctors who speak English impeccably. Several are professionals in other fields. Others are young wives and mothers.
>
> In going back, I was reminded of the two years I taught there, and I hoped that I had [had] a part in the success of these young girls' lives. Then I started thinking about those who've had a part in my life. . . . I knew I needed to thank you. . . . [Y]ou planted a dream in my heart that has been growing ever since. You believed in me. You claimed the best for me. You made me believe I could be anything I wanted to be. And that has made all the difference.
>
> That dream has taken me from my small-town-down-south, provincial world to a world far-reaching: Jordan to Germany, Guatemala to the Gambia. That dream has shaped me from student to teacher to missionary and back again. That dream has challenged me to be the very best person I can be. . . .
>
> You are a teacher, and teachers are leaders, with vision and focus that others of us can follow. Teachers are people of faith, assured of things hoped for, convicted of things not seen. Teachers are nurturers, knowing how to wait—perhaps over long periods of time—to see results. . . . Thank you, Gayle, for being the kind of teacher who is not afraid to invest in the future of a young girl by laying a foundation and planting a dream.

Once again, Paula made me feel brilliant.

The Truths

1. The only really effective teaching I have ever done has been done at someone's elbow, looking into his or her eyes, speaking quietly into his or her ear.

2. The only really significant lesson I have ever taught is "You can do it; I know you can!"—whatever it is that needs to be done at the moment.

3. The most important thing for me to ever understand about my students is that they are unique individuals, that neither I nor anyone can make a silk purse out of a sow's ear (Benny Ray could never be Robert, and Minnie could never be Paula, for countless reasons that can't be changed), but a soft pigskin purse is just as valuable as a silk one, and what looks like a sow's ear might really be a very high grade of cotton or linen that could make something else quite lovely and valuable besides a purse. And the only way to see what a person really is and to help him or her make something of themselves is to look closely at each as a distinctive human being, worth something, worth love and caring and faith.

4. I might have to wait a long, long time to know whether I won one or lost one or was even on the team, and most often I might never know at all, but I *am* a teacher, and teachers *are* people of faith.

5. All things considered, there is no finer way to spend a life. It has made all the difference.

2 May Sheehan

Susan Joan Fishbein
East Meadow High School, East Meadow, New York

Susan Fishbein also remembers an influential individual—the spirited "earth mother" whose twelfth-grade English class inspired her to become a teacher herself, thanks to the rich and lively world of literature it opened up, and who then became the mentor who saw her through that first challenging year in the classroom.

May Sheehan was my twelfth-grade English teacher for English 12A and for "World Drama." She also became my mentor and first supervisor when I returned to the same high school six years after graduating to become an English teacher. She was the reason I did.

Mrs. Sheehan was the first teacher I appreciated in high school for being somewhat mischievous. As a goody-goody student, I found it refreshing and liberating to hear her intimate that there were racy, suggestive things about the lives and works of such authors as Aristophanes, Chaucer, and Shakespeare. She was an Irish earth mother, somewhat plump, but pleasingly so, with twinkling eyes, supple skin, hands that gestured and danced with her musical laughter, and a warm, enveloping smile that made you feel you were her only child, of whom she was ever so proud. Her charm and spirit permeated the classroom, enlivening every discussion and activity, many of which I remember she led. Of course, those were not the days of student-centered instruction; but there was the steady sense that we had been invited to share, on equal footing, the secret thrills of classic literature with May at the helm, always twinkling. In my yearbook she wrote, "Congratulations for a job well done. You gave the greatest pleasure in class, and you'll long be remembered. Love, May Sheehan." No, May, *you* gave the greatest pleasure—that was May, all right, completely self-effacing.

It was May who helped hire me and who guided me through my very shaky (I thought at the time) first year of teaching. I wanted so very much to be just like May, to inhale the sensual pleasures of imagery and motifs, to exhale the excitements of the intellectual senses, and to share those breaths with my students. Having been a top achieving student in her class, I had become her special charge as first-year teacher, and there was much for which she praised me, and in fact, nothing for which she suggested improvement (I think she was quite partial). Through May's encouraging words in her supervisory reports, I gained confidence that perhaps I was, after all, in the right profession, even when plenty of challenges to my authority from undisciplined students made me think otherwise. May wrote in December of my first year that "Your ease in dealing with the students belies your few months in the job. Your students show a respect for your person as well as for your lesson. . . . You appear to be a natural teacher. Your years ahead should be very successful."

When May retired at the end of my first year, I was deeply saddened. My mother helped me find a present for her, an English Toby mug of the Greek god Dionysus. She was thrilled, and I remember her thank-you note mentioning the twinkle in the god's eye that would always watch her from across the room. May was *my* fertility goddess, the being who infused me with a love of teaching, who instilled in me the belief that I could surpass my master/mentor, whose twinkling enthusiasm yet resides in my soul.

3 Human Voice, Wooden Horse

Maureen Neal
Mesa State College

Maureen Neal takes her first mentor's advice and (in addition to refusing to take herself too seriously) looks back over the ups and downs recorded in the green-inked journal she kept during her year of practice teaching in a big-city junior high school.

When I think back to my professional beginnings, my mind focuses on the memory of practice teaching rooted in a big-city junior high school and on a tale of two supervising teachers. One was professional—distant, polite, organized, careful, and competent in every way, including classroom management and discipline. Her students spent a lot of time "on task" in workbooks, study guides, and carefully organized reading assignments. Rules were posted on the blackboard: No Gum, No Food, No Pop Cans, No Chew; No Talking When I'm Talking. She was horrified, and with good reason, to turn over this carefully controlled world to an incompetent—me—for practice teaching.

I also had another supervising teacher who seemed the polar opposite of the first, and her spirit was reflected in her classroom: bulletin boards covered with scraps of student writing; books and loose papers and old *Scholastic* magazines and piles of construction paper filled the bookshelves, falling out of closets; Boggle® and Scrabble® and Probe® games in various states of dilapidation were stored in unlocked cupboards and could be checked out by students who signed up on a list posted inside the cupboard door, no questions asked. What was most revealing was that along the whole length of the window side of the room, geraniums bloomed in pots and jars and ceramic dishes, even coffee cups. This woman, too, was probably reluctant to turn over her world to me for practice teaching—there was such a fine line in her classroom between order and disorder that any outside factor could turn the whole structure on its head and tip the balance, throwing the place into chaos—which is exactly what happened during most of my practice teaching days, as excerpts from my teaching journal will show.

The point I wish to make is that this second supervising teacher made a huge impact on my teaching career, even in whether I would continue in the profession after practice teaching was—mercifully—over. She provided me with a great beginning in the spirit as well as the practice of teaching, and she showed me how to value and to carry those nonquantifiable, immeasurable, completely human things—gut feelings, hunches, intuitions—into the classroom. In other words, maybe great beginnings are not, for some, connected so much to the quality of a teacher preparation program or to the curriculum of a participating school or to the size and location of a chosen school, but to the human beings who are willing to share the teaching/learning environment at its crucial, formative stages.

The person who trusted me with her students and her geranium-filled classroom was Florence Larsen. She gave me lots of advice, even when—*especially* when—I didn't ask for it. Some of the things she told me, I could apply or understand right away. "Your voice gets screechy and shrill when you yell," she said, so I tried to make myself heard quietly. "Don't pride yourself on not sending kids out on referral—sometimes they deserve it," she said, so I sighed and began to send kids down to the principal. "Go out and watch other teachers teaching," she said, so I began to observe what other people did about those things I couldn't figure out or didn't do well—how other teachers led discussion or opened and closed class; how they dealt with fights; how they talked to students in the hall. "First, students have to be able to hear you," she said, which is a deceptively simple and profound piece of advice I still carry in my head.

She also said, "Don't be afraid to show them who you are" and "Don't take yourself so seriously," which may be why I went to my first job being able to tell stories to my students about my two black dogs who ate an entire frozen chicken TV dinner, a pot of spaghetti sauce, a bag of peanuts, and a pair of socks in a wild Halloween rampage; I also disguised myself as one of the Supremes and lip-synched "Stop In the Name of Love" with a group of other teachers for a Christmas talent show. We made shiny, slinky dresses out of Glad® garbage bags, wore our spiked heels on the gym floor, and forgot the words halfway through.

Mrs. Larsen also encouraged me to keep a teaching journal, a record of my practice teaching experience. She pushed me to sort out some of the difficult issues and events by writing through them. "Someday," she said, "you're going to look back at this and laugh at yourself. But you also might learn something, so look at it again in twenty years or so." In hindsight, I am not proud of some of my attitudes, some of the things I did and allowed students to do; I was also naive and arrogant at times. I stumbled, made enough mistakes in judgment to fill a dump truck, and went home from school crying some days. But by writing to her, I also stumbled my way to an understanding of the spirit of teaching and learning that Florence Larsen both embodied and promoted, and so, in her memory, I offer the following excerpts from my 1974 practice teaching journal:

February 11

Today, when Brenda was writing "Peace and Love" and "Romeo and Juliet" on the board, and Peter, my little friend, did not read one word or finish one sentence, and Frankie was out of his seat all day long, and Rudy was punching Annie in the arm and opening the windows and throwing her bobby pins out and stapling the leaves of the plants together, and Carrie and Lisa were yelling and throwing around that little plastic doll, and Robert and Mark and Ernie and Albert were playing tennis with the paper puzzles, and Tommy was throwing the games all over the floor, and Diane was rooting around in the closet, I was just chewing my fingernails and getting mad and stomping on the floor, but I had nothing else for them to do. I was not ready with more. And I would not, even if I could, keep order—something in me refused to do the things I know I need to do. I am the cause of their behavior because I didn't have anything for them to do. I could not believe half the things that happened. I did not expect it or look for it, but it all came crashing down on my head anyway.

If I yell and yell and send referrals and get mad enough to finally make them be quiet, is that the point? But when (if) they ever get quiet, I would still have the problem of not having something for them to do. If they ever ended up ready to listen, would I have anything worthwhile for them to listen to? I doubt it. I'm so confused. I'm spending my days with paper clips in my hair and ditto ink all over my fingers, and I can't seem to think of anything they might want to know.

February 13

I'm writing in green pen because the pens and pencils I take to school seem to disappear without notice. Who would want my chewed-up pen?

I dream about getting hit by flying books and combs stuck in my hair. And the paperwork is what's impossible. I lose my notes to myself, and I lose worksheets and papers and contest forms and excuses, and I run out of pages of things and have to go run some more off in between classes. I am fluttered and flustered.

February 14

Recording small triumphs: Tommy spoke in class discussion today, stopping long enough from hitting the window string against the window and ripping up his book to say he liked the filmstrip. I got along better in seventh hour, and Angela finished two whole questions. Almost got into a fight with Eric over collateral for pencils but finally convinced him I would give back the key chain he was working on. Peter and Albert got valentines in the lunchroom, and this girl threw her tray full of food at another girl who had signed girl number one's name to a valentine. Girl number two sat there with her mouth open, coleslaw dripping off her hair and into her face, food all over the chair and the table and the floor and her clothes. Mr. Perry took them both downstairs.

Don had a good test paper, and I don't know if he copied or not. Even cheating shows some motivation, I suppose. I sent Brenda and Carrie to the Dean today and they deserved it—but the Dean's discipline was for them to write "My education is too valuable and too important to waste my time, my classmates' time, and my teacher's time. My education . . ." over and over, and I was sorry I had sent them. Maybe I am beating them into the ground now, but maybe it's the other way around, too.

February 24

Tonight I feel excited again, ready to go back out into all that confusion, hectic running around with a new frame of mind, something fresh. I feel pretty foolish for worrying so hard, for being so serious, for allowing myself to be so wounded and hurt by mistakes I can't help but make because of my inexperience. I am beginning to realize that my age and lack of experience are uncontrollable factors and that inexperience does not necessarily signify personal failure. By the same token I can't use that inexperience as the excuse to hide behind when I make those mistakes. I'm not learning from mistakes when I get so defensive and threatened by Florence pointing them out to me that I can't even look at her or listen to what she's saying. *I* even stapled the geraniums too, just to show how unhappy I was with the criticism. Now who does that remind you of?

March 4

Today I just decided that I can't put up with all this constant confusion and sense of pushing all the time. I was shocked out of my new quiet shoes today to see Bill with his two black eyes, and to see Lucille with dull and colorless and very unshining eyes, with her real hair and not that wig. In fact, I couldn't believe it was Lucille—but then I knew it had to be by the trademark black jacket, jeans, and white heels. And when she took that cigarette out, I didn't know what I would do next if she lit it in class—she would have a new weapon. And there was a fight in the lunchroom today. While Jack and Debbie, who were on duty, gazed into each other's eyes, some little kid got his teeth kicked in. And all the other teachers had left early, so I walked over, knowing it was going to start, and stood there yelling HEY! HEY! HEY! and stomping my feet wanting to grab one or the other but not wanting *my* orthodontist's teeth to get beat in, too.

It all just seems so sour, so pointless, and I keep thinking that I shouldn't take this so seriously, that this is not as important as I make it out to be. I spend seven hours a day just trying to keep thinking one step ahead of them, and then I come home and grade and record papers and sigh because the highest grade in period seven is 101 points out of 145. And I fill out little attendance and attitude sheets and notes to myself, and I swear to do better next time, and I write notes to kids telling them I like them fine but that I do not like their behavior, and then they sneer at my foolish attempts at communication and sometimes spit on the report cards I spent all night preparing.

March 5

I sent Bill and Arthur and Larry to Mr. Snow at the beginning of the hour. They came back only mildly subdued, and I wonder what they talk about down there. More events: Today I tried a new tactic, and it was kind of hard to do. I tried especially hard not to raise my voice. After Florence telling me three times not to do that, I finally tried it, and instead of trying to yell over their shouts of "Check your*self* out!" I was calm but firm and just kept right on talking quietly. Amazing! They were quiet, but only until they figured out that I had nothing worthwhile to say. Then we had bedlam all over again.

Lisa wrote a note today saying she wished I would shut up, and the next sentence was "I wish there was peace and love over all the earth." Peter sent me a note with a frown face on it, saying, "Why don't you ever come to help *me*?" on it. Carrie had a fight with a boy in the hall, and Danny almost hit Mrs. Shaw. I smiled a big one at Brenda today. (Thought I'd just be completely reckless.) She came up to talk to me twice in the lunchroom.

March 10

You asked me what three things I learned during this experience. Well, a lot more than three things, but I'll be specific. I learned that when you want somebody to be quiet and do some work, one of the things you can do is go over to them and talk to them quietly, that smiling goes a lot further than frowning, that I can't take a key chain away from somebody who's making it for his girlfriend, that if I stand out in the hall with my arms uncrossed more kids will come up and talk to me. I learned to go over to talk to Diane when she's just sitting there doing nothing, waiting to get picked on. I learned to be patient with Roy when he keeps stroking my arm while I am trying to pass out papers in the front of the room, not to let Tommy near the movie projector, and how to stop a fight with my bare hands and a whistle. Do you think these are small potatoes?

March 12

Green pen again. Today was a strangely successful day. In my first two periods we did some Jim Croce stuff. I didn't feel so much like fighting when they would yell out answers to questions—maybe I finally asked a few of the right ones. I think they liked it, even if they would sit and click their tongues and pop their gum at me—when I wasn't looking they would sneak a peek at their sheets, then catch me watching and would be bored again.

Seventh hour was a disaster. First of all I had to send Roy to the library to get the substitute because evidently she hadn't heard the bell ring (twice). I didn't know half the new kids in there, and they tipped over in their chairs five times, so I left (the substitute was in charge) during "Casey at the Bat" to track down lost report cards. When I got back it was a madhouse—no one was paying any attention to the film. So we did report cards but couldn't find honor roll sheets, and so nobody got to be on the honor roll. Then people threw other people's worksheets out the window while the substitute sat at the desk trying to figure out who had been tardy.

March 26

I just want to say thank you for everything—for reading, for listening, for hearing me out even when what I said made no sense. And I learned more in these eight weeks than in four years of school, I think. And I would like to keep in touch, to write September letters about my new job maybe, or about how the new kids don't make me think half as fast as Lucille does when she pulls out her cigarettes. Maybe I'll tell you about how my garden is growing, and I'll ask you about your trip to Sweden, or daughters, or dogs. So thanks again for making me learn things and for letting me make mistakes and for all the help. I needed it.

I began my "real" teaching career in the fall following this practice teaching experience. I taught in a small public high school in Colorado for ten years before moving on to a *very* rural school with a student population of forty students K–12; I also spent a year in a large city high school and worked in an adult continuing education program teaching ESL, GED, creative writing, and introductory composition before enrolling in a Ph.D. program. And though my teaching and educational environments have changed during the course of the past twenty years, I have carried one small thing with me to every new place. It is a little wooden Swedish horse that is hand-painted, mostly orange with some white and red flowers on it. My dog Babe once pulled it from a bookcase and chewed one of its legs and part of its carved tail; a tooth mark lingers near one ear. Florence gave this to me after a trip to Sweden following her retirement, and it is the best thing I have to remind me of the thoughtful and caring beginning she provided me. It now sits near the lamp on my desk at the university office I share with two other graduate students. Occasionally I sigh, tell Florence how I am doing, and ask for her advice. "Don't take yourself so seriously," she says.

4 Some Reflections on Becoming a Teacher

Kenneth Simons
Syosset High School, Syosset, New York

Kenneth Simons describes the transitions he went through in moving from a university to a high school, and from being an Authority with Meanings to transmit to being a facilitator who gives student ways of finding their own—and in the process describes one of the more unusual benefits of having a mentor.

Shortly after completing my graduate work in 1980, I abandoned a fledgling career in college academics to hold several jobs in public relations. In the years before coming to my current job teaching at Syosset High School, I was, in turn, spokesperson for a major utility company, manager of public relations for an airline, and communications director for a law school. I had well-appointed offices, I could more or less control the pace of my day, I had assistants to do the clerical work, and I never even spoke with anyone under the age of twenty-five. These jobs were lucrative, but not once during that period did I feel pleasure or joy in what I'd done during the day. I struggled with the idea of changing careers. Time was running out: I was forty years old and to stay in public relations much longer meant, essentially, a commitment to an unsatisfying career. To switch to teaching meant a big cut in salary and negotiating all the uncertainties such a career change entails. There were other questions. Would I find a teaching job? Was I too set in my ways? What were teenagers like these days . . . ?

Fade to a room full of noisy tenth graders on the first day of school, laughing and shouting, buzzing with nervous expectancy, waiting for me to begin my (unknown to them) first class. Imagine the marvelously comic possibilities—possibilities for well-intentioned but misplaced pedagogical emphases, for ludicrous over- and underestimations of my students, for having my nose rubbed in life. I would like to sketch for you a few of the transitions I experienced in my first years as a teacher. I hope they provoke a smile of recognition in my more experienced colleagues.

Teach Literature Less and Students More

Sometime during the fall of my first year, I scheduled individual writing conferences in my tenth-grade class. I had three sharpened pencils lined up ready to correct comma splices and run-on sentences. A student came up with her paper and sat down at my desk. I had seen the paper in draft form. The child's father, it seems, always wanted sons rather than daughters and made no secret about it. He was distant, cold, and often openly hostile to her sister and her. One day he seemed to relent and bought them a goldfish, which they viewed as a symbol of the love he had withheld. Then the story took an odd turn. The father suddenly usurped the gift he had given; he fed it, played with it, spent time with it. My student felt jealous, thinking that once again something else had taken her place in his affections. Then, just as suddenly, he abandoned the fish. I read further:

> The fish is now twelve inches long and swimming in a tank full
> of algae. My father doesn't have time for it anymore. It isn't spe-
> cial. Swimming in its tank, it is alone. Even though I thought
> one of us was precious to my father, I was wrong. No one could
> replace the son he never had. I am and always will be my
> father's daughter but not his son. I never was and never will be.

I eagerly began to draw editing marks on the page and suggest ways of combining sentences. Then I looked up and realized she was crying. Her back was to the class, and she was embarrassed about being caught in her emotion. So she stared at me, wide-eyed, tears rolling down her cheeks, trying to remain immobile. I looked back down at the paper. I fingered the pencil nervously and tapped the desk a few times. The seconds dragged on. They had not discussed this kind of thing in the teacher-certification courses I'd taken. I smiled lamely. "This is a lovely paper," I said. "Maybe we can talk about it another time." The response was completely inadequate; the words felt inauthentic and thin. She wasn't terribly impressed either. She had revealed something important and intimate. I'd barely noticed, and by the time I did, it was too late. Welcome to your career in teaching.

The notion that there is a strong emotional component to the learning experience of young people came as a surprise to me, as did the recognition that students, rather than literature, should be at the center of the curriculum. University instruction—the only model I had had to draw upon at that point—largely discounts both. I taught freshman English as a graduate instructor. No one ever said a word about using what the students learned—rather than what I taught—as the standard of measurement for a successful class. I took my teaching assignments very seriously, but viewed them as secondary to the task of research and of carving out an academic niche, and I believe my attitude reflected the prevailing view of teaching at the university. Only once, during a two-hour doctoral oral exam, was I asked a question about how I might teach a novel.

Given this background, I struggled in my early lessons with the problem of providing meaningful pathways for students to respond to fiction and poetry, particularly in their writing. Although it's essential for students to relate the literature to their lives, I felt efforts at relevance that trivialized the text (". . . if you invited Romeo and Juliet to your birthday party . . . ") were misguided and did more harm than good. Gradually I began to see that one productive solution lay in broadening the definition of text rather than seeking artificially low experiential grounds for student response. Cartoons, advertisements, paintings, clothing, and, in some instances, rock videos can legitimately be considered texts and valid occasions for "reading." Like all texts, these are systems of formal relationships that can be described; they contain meanings that can be interpreted and articulated. The benefit, obviously, is that they are linked directly with the students' experience and therefore allow them to use what they already know, sometimes in exceptionally sophisticated ways.

For example, in a senior class we were considering taped television advertisements as texts and discussing how the various elements of the ads function together to form a meaning. One group of students examined a Nissan automobile ad that was intended to show the merits of the 1992 model cars prior to the arrival of the 1993 model. A print graphic that read "Hasta la vista, Baby" flashed on the screen for perhaps a second in the middle of the ad. The graphic had no apparent relationship to other words and images in the text. When asked what it might be doing there, students immediately identified it as a line from the film *Terminator II*. They were then able to interpret the ad entirely on their own: The film is about the superiority of an older model machine over a newer, more sophisticated one. Therefore the graphic served as a reinforcement for the meaning of the ad as a whole, which it recapitulated. The literary concepts we were working with here—metaphor, metonymy, allusion, the intentionality of meaning—were transparently clear in this format. Most important, the students were able to produce an interpretive text on their own, rather than simply replicate a model proposed by the teacher.

I don't mean to impugn the role of traditionally studied texts. We read about eight major pieces of literature in class each year, and it's important for students to be exposed to these. After all, cultural literacy is part of our mission, and students are not going to live their lives in the world of television advertising. My point is that a powerful shift took place in my own intellectual values and priorities. I moved from asking questions that presupposed a specific answer to providing students with strategies for asking their own questions; from teaching a work as having a particular "content" to giving students keys to the taxonomic hierarchy and freeing them to arrive at their own conclusions; in short, from being an Authority who doles out Meaning to a facilitator who enables students to discern and make their own. Many of the pieties of the critical and academic traditions on which I cut my teeth gave way before the actual learning needs of students, and this was a wonderfully liberating experience.

A Good Mentor Is Hard to Find

For reasons that will become clear, I very much regret the fact that New York's Mentor Intern program was eliminated in 1992 as part of the state's effort to cope with fiscal problems. The program, which had been in existence for five years, provided release time for master teachers to work directly with beginners on matters of daily concern, such as class management, creating valid forms of assessment, and so forth. The aim of the program was to reduce the very high rate of attrition among first-year teachers (in the late 1980s, approximately 50 percent of new teachers left the profession after one year), and all indications are that it fulfilled its purpose. The program provided the kind of practical support that dramatically reduces frustration and increases efficiency. I can say categorically that my life as a first-year teacher would have been more difficult and my classroom performance even less effective were it not for the day-to-day advice of my mentor. While building administrators gave me very positive guidance on issues such as my questioning technique or designs for cooperative learning, she helped me with the daily intricacies of the job that experienced teachers no longer even notice: how to arrange seating; the principles and etiquette of parent conferences; decoding teenage behavior; how to set up a gradebook so that I was able to make sense of the thing.

Not surprisingly, one of the topics we discussed most often was the overall lack of coordination between the training courses required for a teaching license and the realities of the classroom. This hardly comes as a revelation, but I do feel the time is approaching when collectively we will have to acknowledge that in no other profession is there a wider gap between practice and theory and is theory itself less systematized. To some extent any profession is defined by a central core of ideas and methods, and training in them doesn't stray far from a realistic model: to become an attorney, you read case law; to become an M.D., you study the anatomy of real people. Yet in our profession, which is as important as either of these, we don' t look at the classroom holistically with an eye toward practice. Piaget and Kohlberg are engaging thinkers, but their practical application could be explained in an hour. To ask prospective teachers to "study" them is to invest too much credibility in what amounts to nomenclature. In effect, institutions that certify teachers are saying, "Okay, now you know in principle why Bobby is acting out, but you can discover on your own how to get him to love a book." I'm hoisted with my own petard here, because frankly I don't have a practical suggestion to redress this imbalance in the direction of theory. But certainly a challenge we face together is designing thorough, subject-specific methods courses to facilitate good teaching and enrich the lives of our students.

In lieu of these, the best instruction for me was observing my mentor. Her classroom demeanor was relaxed, friendly, polished, and seemingly effortless. Her classes were well-behaved. Boys removed their hats when they entered the room. When an occasional problem arose, the culprit could be stopped instantly by a silent stare that by a practiced alchemy became a smile just as quickly. The students understood and enjoyed their roles, working diligently and happily. She moved the class toward serious academic goals but with a light touch, stopping here to examine a side issue, pausing there to joke and regroup before going on. But what most impressed me in those early days was not her academic ability, however considerable. I was simply astonished at the extent to which her students wanted to be around her, and how much of themselves they brought to her outside of the purely academic student-teacher relationship. They came to her office during her free periods to discuss books they were reading and films they'd seen. They sat with her in the hall during her duty period to talk about problems with friends, fears about the future, prom dresses. (I assure you, my students did not then seek me out during their free time.) I dimly saw that this magnetism, employed in a different way, was the key to success in the classroom. Part natural ability and part practice, it opened the students to the experience of learning. In any case, to use it constructively, to reach the head through the heart and the heart through the head, is a sign of true mastery. I was deeply impressed. I thought the matter over very carefully and at great length. After a year, I married her.

5 A Great Beginning: My Personal Journey

Donald M. Shafer
Fairview High School, Fairview Park, Ohio

Donald M. Shafer recalls the mentor whose advice and encouragement helped shape his career, and he reflects more broadly on the important place that his experience and his reading of the literature have led him to assign acting while mentoring in his own role as department chair.

I remember my first day as an English teacher just as if it were last week. It wasn't. It has been twenty-six years since that beginning— a "great beginning"! Since then, I have remained a classroom teacher, and I am currently a department chair.

After serving an interim job with the state welfare agency, in January of 1968 I inquired at the local board of education to see whether a job was available at midyear in English teaching. I talked to the superintendent and was offered a junior high position. My job orientation was a short talk with the principal two days before I started, but we formed a friendship that lasted for the next six years. From that first meeting, my great beginning and subsequent career in education began. I didn't know it then, but the principal was to become my mentor, an idea I didn't understand until twenty years later while writing my dissertation. I realized that Bill Leighty, my principal, guided me through my first few years in education, giving me valuable advice and encouragement while at the same time guiding my career.

About three months into the job, Bill called me into his office for a talk. He started the meeting by telling me that he thought I was a natural in the classroom, and he recommended that the superintendent renew my contract for the following year. I only had to enroll for six semester hours to reapply for a temporary certificate, since I was not yet certified. My mentor gave me more good counsel by advising me to start my master's degree program and to fulfill the certification requirements at the same time, especially if I thought I was going to stay in education.

The following fall, after my first courses in education, I started the year with vigorous idealism and boundless energy. I became a "true believer" in the power of education to give students the tools to pursue a better life and to shape mushy minds into thinking organs. My dream was to take each student to a higher plain. Since I was not shy about trying new things, and being puffed up by the confidence my mentor displayed in me, I began making changes in my classroom that differed from the way English was taught in the rest of the building. I put grammar on the back burner, had students write full compositions, and established a paperback book club. The students were enthusiastic, and parents began to notice the changes. They made favorable comments to the principal and the superintendent.

Sometime during that year, our staff was taken to Centerville, Ohio, to examine two educational innovations: the middle school idea and team teaching. With the courses I was taking at the university, I began a serious study of these new directions. My enthusiasm was whetted more when I learned that the junior high building in which I was teaching was to become a middle school the following year. My passion was so great that I talked a couple of colleagues into trying team teaching for that year. When my colleagues and I went to the principal and told him we wanted to institute team teaching and mini-courses in English, his comment was short and to the point: We were to submit a plan so that he could adjust the schedule for next year. He was as excited as I was about the possibilities.

The following September, Bill invited me into his office for another one of his talks. He wanted me to be on the curriculum council for the school district. He explained that the curriculum council reviewed program changes that affected the district. After I agreed to be on the council, he asked about my courses at the university and recommended that I study curriculum and supervision with an emphasis on English. Bill encouraged me by saying that he believed I would be excellent in curriculum innovation and in leading change. A dream was beginning to take shape.

I followed Bill's advice, which was sound counsel, and started my major in curriculum and supervision. When, the following June, the coordinator of language arts in the district resigned, Bill called me into his office and encouraged me to apply. I was shocked because I was not officially certified as a teacher, and I didn't think I had the experience for that position. After more exhortations from him, I applied and was hired. I knew it was his hand that had helped me to get the position.

Throughout the next two years, I found myself in many different leadership roles. I left the middle school and started teaching high school. Then, in 1974, I moved to the Cleveland area to become a department chair. I never found another Bill Leighty to advise me or give me the same kind of career assistance or counsel. In fact, I began to realize the value of having a mentor like Bill. No one in my new district helped or even cared like my old principal.

Some years later, I realized what Bill Leighty had done for me and what a mentor does to promote a career. While looking for a dissertation topic, I stumbled upon a book by Daniel J. Levinson entitled *The Seasons of a Man's Life.* Since I was approaching late summer or early autumn in my own life, the book appealed to me. Levinson wrote about the mentor relationship and its impact on the men he had studied. He discovered that the many successful men who had developed mentor relationships were fortunate indeed. Levinson found evidence to suggest that the mentor enhanced the protégé's skills and intellectual development. The mentor used his influence to facilitate the young colleague's entry and advancement in a profession and acquainted him with the career's values, customs, resources, and cast of characters. Additionally, the mentor provided counsel and moral support, and what is more important supported and facilitated the realization of a dream or the perception that the young adult had of himself and his life's goals (Levinson 1978, 23).

Another book put it a different way. In *Effective Teaching and Mentoring,* Laurent A. Daloz summed up the idea of dreams and mentors using words from Bruno Bettelheim. Bettelheim wrote that mentors remind us that we can indeed survive the journey of early adulthood and undergo transformation by moving through, not around, our fears. Mentors give us the magic that allows us to enter the darkness, a talisman to protect us from evil spells, a gem of wise advice, a map, and sometimes courage. The mentor appears near the outset of the journey as a helper, equipping us in some way for what is to come (Daloz 1986, 17).

After reading these two books, I kept returning to the authors' words about dreams and the metaphor of the journey. Upon reflection, I came to understand their importance. My first principal, Bill Leighty, helped me shape my dream and set me on my journey. I knew before I started teaching that I wanted to be in service to humankind. Bill helped me shape a vague notion into concrete reality. However, he did more than shape my dream. He assisted me in my journey from classroom teacher, to coordinator of language arts, to department chair. He encouraged me along the way and transformed my fears and doubts into accomplishment and higher self-esteem.

From these books and other mentoring literature, I came to realize the power of the mentor. It is not the same kind of power usually associated with the word, but it is the power to quietly affect another's career by helping with his or her journey and assisting in the fulfillment of that person's dreams. It has been through my personal experience of being mentored and my study of the benefits of mentoring that I have tried to give new educators a "great beginning" like the one given to me. The power of mentoring is extraordinary and should be a part of everyone's life and career. The beginning educator has much to navigate when starting out. I hope I can give the novice the same sound advice and guidance that was given to me. I firmly believe that the greatest gift the supervisor, department chair, or coordinator can give to a novice is that of a mentor first and a supervisor last.

By the way—thank you, Bill, for my great beginning!

References

Daloz, Laurent A. 1986. *Effective Teaching and Mentoring: Realizing the Transformational Power of Adult Learning Experiences.* San Francisco: Jossey-Bass.

Levinson, Daniel J. 1978. *The Seasons of a Man's Life.* New York: Ballantine.

6 Having Seized the Day—and Let Go

Diana Wagner Marmaluk
Beaver College

Diana Wagner Marmaluk remembers both what made her want to be a Teacher with a capital T and why she felt she could no longer teach in the sixth-grade urban classroom where she had struggled for three years to make a difference.

Two weeks after seeing Robin Williams yell *"Carpe diem"* in *Dead Poets' Society*, I walked into my first homeroom: a sixth-grade, parochial urban classroom. Not exactly a boarding school in the country for rich kids. But then, I'm not exactly Robin Williams. The graffiti outside my new school didn't throw so much as a shadow over me as I hung giant punctuation marks from the ceiling. My confidence and excitement alone, I thought, would carry me gracefully into the lives of these children, who so far existed only on a roll sheet. I would make these children love language, love learning, and I—unlike Robin Williams—wouldn't need to stand on desks or tear up textbooks to do it. I was a Teacher. And I came into a system that I believed wanted to nurture the kind of teacher I am.

After the euphoria of the first day and the start of a full week of classes, I realized that being in the school system would test—and ultimately conquer—my perseverance in two main areas: work load and attention to *teaching*.

I taught six periods per day—no prep time, a half hour for lunch, after-school carpool supervision. My preps numbered eight: three sections of English, two sections of computer science, one biology, one earth science, and one cross-graded reading class (made up of three levels). I learned quickly that the only way to fulfill testing requirements (four test grades per quarter, per child, per subject) was to make short quizzes, to grade them in class, and to make sure I asked the questions the curriculum required. The boss from the main office would be by one day to check the numbers.

Even when I kept the numbers flowing in my grade book, I was frustrated by the decreasing amount of time I actually spent teaching.

While discipline in my classroom was never a problem, I sometimes had to interrupt class to pull sweating, bleeding, cursing eighth-graders off each other as they tangled in the hallway outside my cracked door. I never kept track of—or caught up to—the many students who missed class because they were warming the principal's bench, on suspension, truant, or hiding in the bathroom. It was enough to keep track of the 112 different faces who came in and went out of my room every day.

Several times that first year, I spent morning time washing children whose uniforms were still stained with the sweat of last week's gym class, or splitting my donut with the little one who always came to school hungry. (She carried an empty lunch box so as to appear like the rest.) I sometimes spent after-school time consoling the child who thought he was dumb because when he wrote, all of his letters came out backwards. I bandaged knees, supervised detention, and always spent part of my lunch hour reminding my group of boys of the penalty for throwing peanut butter in the girls' hair.

So I was a Teacher. The first year. The second. The third. Enough. I wasn't teaching by now; I was fighting. I looked forward to the traffic jams on the interstate just so I could release the day's tears: for the principal who didn't want to "make trouble" for the abusive parent; for the teacher who told me not "to bother" with a field trip to Edgar Allan Poe's house; for the child who read Shel Silverstein, smiled, sat straight, and then frowned, slouched, and said, "Poetry's stupid."

Nearly two years after leaving that place, with its yellow walls and its Crayola® attempts to belie the neighborhood's scorn of learning, I still spend about one afternoon a month writing letters back to several of my former students. They still ask, "Why did you go?"

"Time to move on, pal."

"Are you coming back?"

"Don't think so."

"Oh."

These few correspondents were the ones I loved there. They are the ones who, in their prepubescent bashfulness, loved me and understood me as more than their teacher. They understood me as a Teacher. Their question *Why did you go?* leads me to the more pressing question: What could have made me stay?

A supportive peer environment would have made a difference. Rather than responding to my early enthusiasm with comments like "You'll get *that* out of your system," senior faculty members—if they had received early encouragement and support—could have helped me set realistic goals in this very challenging environment. The principal, from whom attitudes seemed to flow, could have given me and my peers ample feedback and positive encouragement to help us build on our successes and tackle our challenges.

Collaboration in matters concerning curriculum, testing, and discipline would have given all of us in that school ownership of the processes that directed our students. We then would have had greater community ownership of our individual successes and greater accountability for our individual failures.

If I could offer advice to any new teacher, it would be to find a supportive peer and develop a collegial, confident trust with that person. Stay away from the burn-outs. Stay away from the people hanging on only because they'll qualify for retirement in a few more years. Let your principal know when something works well. Send that "problem child" down to the office with a note of praise when he aces his spelling test or makes it through the morning without giving someone the elbow.

Share your successes. Share your fears. Remind yourself early and often each day of the student who always gives you her undivided attention, begs to wash your boards, and walks you to your car when you have too much to carry. Learn that when you "give up" part of a Saturday to read the poem by the boy who never smiles and never sits still, you're not "giving up" anything. You're simply trading gifts. And never, ever cry on the expressway unless traffic is jammed.

In this small school of nine teachers, I began my first year as one of three novices. At the end of the third year, I was the only one left. The others said, "Why bother?" early on. I, at least, waited until I had forgotten why I bothered in the first place.

Now that my junior high experience is well behind me, I remember why I bothered. I remember why I still choose to capitalize *Teacher*. Their names are Hank and Megan and Jen and Kelly and Kimmy and Danny. . . .

Carpe diem.

7 The Road Taken, Gladly

Wang Zhijun
Huazhong University of Science and Technology, People's
Republic of China

*Wang Zhijun movingly recalls how her growth as a teacher has paralleled
the growth of the students she teaches in her native China, in the process
describing how she has learned to be much more than the "schoolmarm" her
society might label her, by encouraging her students to be active in their
own learning.*

I had never dreamed of becoming a teacher before I was admitted to a teachers' college, which I entered with great reluctance and little alternative. I was afraid it was my last chance to get any college education after more than ten years of deprivation during Mao's Cultural Revolution. Something in me was touched, nonetheless, by a film I had seen a few days before, *A Village Teacher,* in which the title character devoted all of her life to children in the countryside.

Being a shy, reserved person, I was so self-conscious while giving my first class as a practice teacher that there seemed to be a slight mistiness preventing me from seeing clearly either the faces of the pupils, the teachers, and my classmates sitting at the back of the classroom, or my carefully prepared lesson plan. Fortunately, I was too lacking in self-confidence not to have learned by heart every word of the plan, so I would be able to speak as required even in case of nervousness. Things went smoothly, as planned, and I was praised. But in fact, I felt as if I were doing things in my sleep. Ten years later, a classmate from those days told me: "You conducted the class with a blank expression. I really couldn't understand how you should get praised!"

It was with even greater reluctance that I took an appointment to teach the English language in a middle school after graduation, for I liked studying better than teaching, and I wanted to pursue advanced study; at least, I thought, I ought to be given a position in some college according to my school record. I might not have received the job but for the affable, thoughtful headmaster, who was a representative of the National People's Congress (somebody corresponding to an MP). She saw through me at first sight and tactfully awakened something in my nature and persuaded me successfully.

The first class I gave in the middle school was attended by some elderly teachers there, who sang high praise for my English. This calmed me down, and I became brave enough to take some glances at my pupils when I began teaching as a real teacher. In one of the two classes under my instruction were some very difficult boys, whose mischievous behavior not only gave their teacher a headache but also caused their own failure in their studies. Quite a few people, including myself, doubted whether I could get them under control, since it was obvious that I was the same kind-hearted, good-tempered, and smiling-faced sort of person as the teacher whom I had replaced. But to my surprise, the whole class listened to me so attentively that I could see an interested look in every child's face. I read in their eyes that they were touched by my words, my English, my amiability, and my enthusiasm, and when our eyes met, a spark of communication linked our hearts—we, pupils and teacher, began to share something, and it is this *something* that has bound us together ever since. Thus my career began.

My pupils were first-year students in junior middle school, at the age of about twelve. Maybe this is the most difficult time for young boys. However, I seemed to enjoy the tricks they played, whereas some regarded them as serious problems. Perhaps my feelings were the result of having been a "good" child, one too obedient and well-behaved to develop a child's instinct naturally. I watched them playing, laughing, shouting, and jumping about, and could not help smiling at such a picture of happy childhood. The boys and girls in my middle school were sensitive to kind feelings. As a result, they soon felt an attachment to me. They never felt nervous in my class. Whenever we met, they would greet me with hearty, broad smiles. These smiles, in turn, made me feel attached to those lovely pupils. I felt I had the ability as well as the responsibility to improve their English study.

I found that those who played tricks in class were not dull pupils. On the contrary, some of them were fairly clever, too clever to sit still listening to a teacher's repeated explanations, for they were able to catch what was said the first time, even while playing with something. But they were too young to tell the reason why. That is a teacher's duty. A language teacher should not dwell upon some point for an unnecessarily long time without giving the pupils an opportunity to practice. Although everyone knows "practice makes perfect," many, both teachers and students, take it for granted that the more hardworking a teacher is, the more he or she should be engaged in talking. Many teachers order the pupils to put their hands behind their backs so as to keep them from playing with things. I did not. Instead, I asked them to take notes, to consult dictionaries, to read after me, to practice pattern drills, to answer my questions one by one—I kept them busy in class from beginning to end. I kept watching those particularly restless ones and surprised them by questioning them the moment I finished some instruction. To keep them concentrating, I deliberately gave them harder tasks, and they liked such challenges and felt proud of meeting them. To those who did have difficulties, I usually made things easier by asking them simpler questions, giving them more time for preparation, inviting them to repeat quicker pupils' answers, and so on. To arouse their interest, I read them amusing or attractive English stories with impressive intonation, taught them English songs, or helped them to put on short English plays. Sometimes we played language games together. My classes became so lively and interesting that studying English became great fun for those boys and girls. After class, they usually chose to do my assignments before any other homework. Once, after three days' absence due to illness, when I appeared at the door of the classroom, they burst out in loud applause with acclamations. My pupils cheerfully hailed me, and some of the more ill-behaved boys even jumped with joy from their seats. When the bell rang and I stood in front of the chalkboard and greeted them, they answered my greeting in such strong voices and in such high spirits that we all laughed, happily and heartily.

In two years' time, the students made remarkable progress: Their average scores rose from 60 to 80. For them, it was many steps forward, and for me, it meant 20 scores multiplied by 120 pupils—2,400 steps in all. The success filled my pupils and me with pride and confidence.

Later, I transferred to another middle school to teach seniors. These teenaged students were physically and psychologically different. Some of them were instinctively eager to show their independence in thought and action. They began to consider it shameful to obey orders too readily. They no longer wanted to be treated as children and tried to keep themselves from being attached to anyone (though, in fact, they still showed such a tendency). They were at the age of seeking some ideal being to worship. I know I could not "convert" them unless I proved worthy of their "conviction." But now I was confident that I could win their obedience, because I was already sure of my teaching abilities and methods. My English was as good as (if not better than) that of the best teachers they had ever had, and I had read enough to invite their questions. I was able to make difficult things easier for them to understand, learn, and memorize. I organized classes in an active way so that the students could learn what was taught in class, and homework was just a written practice extending from class as a kind of review. Differing opinions were encouraged. If I made any slips of the tongue or pen, I would admit the mistakes sincerely. In public, I carefully avoided hurting their dignity while pointing out their errors. However, I didn't let anyone off easily, especially those who neglected their studies. I would criticize such students severely (but usually in private), and some of them would admit their mistakes with tears in their eyes. I always reminded them of their responsibility as seniors, family members, and citizens of China. Their sense of responsibility, together with mine, played a very important role in our English teaching and learning. We achieved as much as the "best" classes, but in less time. Besides, my students showed stronger abilities in speaking, listening, reading, and writing, and especially in quick response, although some of their skills were not exhibited in their written examinations. The achievement I took the greatest pride in was their ability at self-teaching, which I spent the most time on, and spared no efforts in cultivating. I am afraid that many teachers forget to cultivate this ability. They habitually force their students to sit silently, listening to many "what's," "why's," and "how's" about the language, hour after hour. While they exhaust themselves by speaking, the students become sleepy from mere listening. I never provided my students with ready conclusions before helping them to find useful expressions, special idioms, new structures, and grammatical rules for themselves. I refused to answer questions that could be answered by simply consulting a dictionary. I tried to plunge my students into the sea of language by involving them in a variety of language activities, so as to enable them to swim by their own effort as much as possible. I believe that they will retain a great deal of what they learned. Elaborate explanations are only necessary when they are used to help, rather than replace, the learning of the language.

I never lost my temper, except once. That was with those ill-behaved juniors. For what reason, I've forgotten. But I will never forget the result: When I spoke to them angrily, they burst into one fit of laughter after another, and at last, I could not keep myself from laughing either. That ended my first and last "violent rage." I cannot remember what I said then, but the laughing faces remain clear in my mind and help to calm me down whenever I feel like flying into a passion. In fact, a peaceful and poised atmosphere was more effective. No one contradicted me in or out of class. It was not that they didn't dare, but that they felt the study of English was our common task to be fulfilled through mutual efforts. They would be sorry for what I expressed sorrow over, and I would be as overjoyed as they at any advance they made.

My middle school teaching experience has proven valuable during the years that I have been teaching at the college level. I've been getting along fairly well with the young adult students because I know what they were like during their junior and senior middle school days, just as a mother knows every detail of her daughter's or son's childhood. I also know what should be taught: I skip what they've already learned, review some points they are apt to forget, and add something important that is not elaborated in the textbook. But the most important (or maybe the most troublesome) thing of all is that I have to train them from the very beginning: I tell them how to take notes, encourage them to speak English in class, "force" them to answer my questions—(In China, it seems that a good class should be a quiet one, and students are trained to keep their mouths tightly shut, waiting for the teacher to give answers. Foreign teachers in China often have great difficulty getting responses from students, especially college students.)—and even correct some of their errors in writing English letters, such as "t," "r," and "b." At first, a few students usually show some impatience with these detailed requirements in study habits, but before long they realize that I am teaching them not only the language, but also the correct ways to gain knowledge, and that is all the more valuable and will prove beneficial in their future study, work, and life.

Through observation and communication, I understand that "adults" though they be (more exactly, old teenagers), they still need very much care, though in a hidden way. I let each of them feel that he or she is my special concern. This is not at all some "tact" or "strategy." Since each one has his or her own advantages and disadvantages, strong points and shortcomings, it is necessary and practical to give everyone individual attention. In addition, I want their English study to always be associated with a kind of warm and pleasant feeling that will help them remember with accuracy what they learned in class.

I compare their many years of study in school with the building of a ship, and college study with the final equipment, before they set sail on the boundless ocean of knowledge and life. I tell them that that's why I demand that they solve problems on their own. I let them know that they will do better, and sometimes that they are already doing better than I am, especially at some creative work that needs youthful originality and inspiration. I show genuine interest in listening to their different opinions, and express my hope that some day we can discuss texts and exercises instead of the present tell-and-listen, ask-and-answer class patterns. I'm pleased to notice that although they are "sophisticated" enough to tell lies readily, my students always tell me the truth in spite of knowing that they may get criticized for it.

When I see my students grow up both physically and spiritually, or read such overflattering words in their letters or greeting cards as "You are a beautiful teacher—We all love you," "I admire you for your profound knowledge and extensive learning, refined humor, and grace," or "You are the first I've ever met who works so selflessly," I feel a little intoxicated with something I'm not certain of. But one thing is certain: I've met the challenge, proven my ability, and most significant of all, gained confidence.

Nevertheless, my gain is not without pain and loss. While I have spent my time, energy, and intelligence on others' children, some of my former schoolmates have successfully gained things for themselves: master's or doctoral degrees, money, comfortable lives. . . .

> I shall be telling this with a sigh . . .
> Two roads diverged in a wood, and I— . . .

In China, there are some nicknames for teachers, such as "schoolsmith" and "kids' king," implying teaching is but an occupation no better than that of a blacksmith or a carpenter. But I'm convinced that teaching is a profession that requires a noble mind, a kind heart, and a strong will, in addition to intelligence, originality, perseverance, a wide range of knowledge . . . and, if possible, some sense of humor.

May it come true in China and the whole world someday that "Teaching is the most admirable profession under the sun."

8 This Is Not about Dreams

Julia M. Emig
The Bridge School, Chelsea, Massachusetts

In this poetic and plainspoken memoir, Julia Emig writes of the dreams and hard realities the new teacher lives as she learns to confront the pain engendered both by "the reality that we have very little control" and at the same time by "how much control we do have."

A Student Makes a Choice

"You shouldn't be a teacher," the roughened Manhattan eighth grader warns. He is eating his lunch—a bag of barbecue potato chips.

"Why not?" I ask. It is only my second day of student teaching.

"Because you have to put up with kids like me who cut class."

"At least I give you an option. Because I choose to teach, you have a choice: to cut or not to cut." Mr. Barbeque just laughs at me and shrugs off. "Did I really say that?" I think to myself. "Is this some holy garden of paradise in which God has created school, a tree of knowledge, so that people may have a choice about the apple?" I catch myself, reminded of the apple those students would bring to their beloved teacher, Ms. Crabtree, in *The Little Rascals*. I want to run after Mr. Barbecue and make him choose to give me an apple. So my career has finally begun—shouldn't there be music playing somewhere?

Macbeth

I am in charge of the eighth graders for the second time. Three of them are busy videotaping me from the corner of the classroom so that I can present the tape to my student teaching seminar later that day. At the time, I do not realize that they are not only videotaping me, but also the bell schedule on the wall, the woman walking her dog outside the window, a can of Ajax® in the back of the room. "Be sure to wash with Ajax," one of them whispers into the recorder attached to the camera. My own voice comes swimming through as I struggle to make Macbeth's dilemma come alive for my students.

"Is there anything you'd die for?" I ask. Many students say that they would die for freedom and family. A few say that they are incapable of answering such a question and are angry at me for bringing it up. Two students say that they would give their lives to go to certain schools, to become professionals. Their classmates give them a hard time for feeling this way. I tell them that in reality, these choices give us insight into Macbeth. "What options do we have in our culture? Macbeth's choices were framed within the structure of monarchy. For some of us today, good schools and certain vocations are what we are taught to value. This has an impact on all of us." The video camera zooms in on my nose.

"No, Ms. English Teacher," says a student. "Macbeth is under the spell of Lady Macbeth. And when she dies, she will kill God with Macbeth's dagger and take over the world."

This student is worried about graduating and getting into the high school of his choice. I laugh with my students at the image of Lady Macbeth terrorizing heaven, but I do not respond. It's a helpless feeling, much like the one I had when the Rodney King verdict erupted. I tell my students that they may choose for themselves who they wish to be. They tell me that Lady Macbeth is queen of the universe and ask me to explain the United States judicial system.

Another student says, "Macbeth has a dagger in his mind. Isn't his choice kind of a suicide, either way?"

Sunsets

Eighth graders are scattered along the floor outside of the art room. The landscape paintings all contain the following: one blot of yellow sun, a green strip of earth, and a blue ribbon of sky. I kneel next to an artist. "Have you ever looked at the sky?" I ask her.

"Sure," she says with hesitation.

"What does it look like today?"

"I don't know," she giggles. "I rode the subway this morning. Besides, I'm too tired to look at the sky at 7:30."

I remember one of my art teachers insisted that we draw each other's faces without looking at the drawing. She said that we have trained ourselves to represent reality in very unreal ways. "You must sketch with a blind eye to your drawing," she dictated.

The hardest lessons to teach are those that I am trying so hard to learn myself.

In Spite of

I cling to Robert Coles's *The Call of Stories* as though it were a bar grip on the subway. I read it between college and school, between school and Brooklyn, between Brooklyn and home. I need to hear Coles's story of his apprentice years. He feels as insecure as I do now. I find myself curling up at the base of what is old and familiar, like the taste of baby aspirin in my throat when I'm sick.

Not that I feel sick. Whenever I step out of the shower in the morning, I spread my arms out and whisper to the dorm's antifungal curtain, "I am beginning." There is a gloss of water on my new skin. I slap myself awake with coffee and the voice of my education professor: "Create yourself new as a young teacher. You survived in spite of your education. Don't look back."

I sketch a picture of myself with a blind eye to my drawing. I sketch again and again. Is this the one I want to be?

Fantasy

I try on many identities. I walk along Park and 82nd, thinking about what it would be like to experience the lifestyle of a kept woman. What if I were one? I'd go home to one of those penthouses and have an affair with the determination that comes whenever we do what we have to do in order to survive. I don't want a romance. I want to harness the possibility to choose to be an entirely different kind of person, one whose perspective on that first cup of coffee in the morning can change at will. I want to die satisfied that I've been many different people.

The Plastic Surgeon

Once, I watched a television talk show that featured people who had physical deformities. One woman's face stopped short below her mouth, much like a Fisher-Price® toy. She said that children would follow her home from school, throwing rocks at her face and hurling insults. A couple of women were bald and wore wigs to hide their secret. Many had tried to alter their appearances unsuccessfully.

One of the guest speakers was a plastic surgeon. He said that he didn't invent the world, that people were only natural in their desires to blend, and that he had helped hundreds of people into healthier lives. "Don't give people an excuse to use your deformity against you," he said. The women on the panel fought back, demanding that people become more accepting of them. Why should they have to change to look like everyone else? *What if the changes didn't work?*

Do I teach my students to write, read, speak, truly *think*, to force them to conform to some greater reality? "Yes," I say to them, "you need to know how to put a sentence together to get a job. You need to know how to look and act educated. Lack of education is a deformity, and people can use it against you." I am a plastic surgeon, promoting the educated "look" so that my students can be mainstreamed into life. The idea is bittersweet, outlining the tension in my dreams. Don't we all wish to be thousands of different people before we die?

Dream

As a new teacher, I catch every possible germ. I'm still building up the appropriate antibodies. During a bad case of the flu, I had a fever dream. I was in my hometown, trying to find my way though a neighborhood I did not recognize. I got lost in the slums. There were streets lined with abandoned schoolhouses made of steel and concrete. I peeked into one. There were rows of lockers, like soldiers standing guard. The dream disintegrated into the crumbling remains of my old high school outdoor stadium, a private Roman ruin. I did not feel young back then. *I survived in spite of my education.* A sketch of myself appeared in the distance, and I remembered just in time to turn a blind eye.

I tell a friend of mine about the dream. She reverses the tables. After all, her mother has been teaching for years. "It's funny you should tell me about your dream," she says, "because I had a dream about you. You were buying stale donuts in your underwear. You were worried about failing something. But it's okay. I don't want you to worry. I can control my dreams. My mother says to teach is to live."

I go to bed that night thinking about what it must be like to have such control while being asleep. I decide to dream about the warm breath of Icelandic sheep, a red tulip garden, and a solidified identity as a teacher. Instead I dream I'm buying donuts in my underwear.

When another friend calls the next evening and says, "I had a dream about you," I tell him no.

"Why? This is a good dream. You were autographing books of poetry in a dimly lit bookstore. I was waiting for you to notice me, and when you did, you smiled. I'm sure you're a wonderful teacher. But there must be more . . . ?"

Yes, there is more! I am a thousand different people. I think about what it must be like to have the life of a poet, to know that introspection and silk-spun words buy the bread. The challenge to blindly sketch one-self is a personal battle for the poet; teaching is so damn public.

The Colleague

I embark on a new journey and take a job teaching high school. One of the first remarks I hear is from a colleague who jokes about kicking students to make them behave. His humor saves him from himself, and I like him best when he can comfortably stand outside the window of my classroom door and make faces at my students. We all share a laugh when this happens. I have the unique perspective of sharing my students' generation; most of my colleagues are at least one generation ahead of me.

A problem arises when said colleague bursts into the classroom and lets fire a string of angry words, some obscene, at me and my students because of my inability to manage the classroom properly. "I have to talk to you later about some ideas for running this class," he surges and proceeds to damn my students to hell.

I would never say that his wrath is entirely undeserved. I am struggling over these very issues of classroom management, the part of teaching that everyone says a new teacher can only experience in order to learn. Does detention really solve problems? Why can't they sit on the tables? I spent my formative years perched on tables in classrooms. (I survived in spite of the system, right?) I can't blame my students for being more interested in what's happening on the other side of the window at times. I can see how many of them are consumed by the chaos of their own lives, their own desires to be thousands of different people.

The Student Who Crossed the Line

One of my students published her drawing of a nude woman in the high school literary magazine. Flowers grew around the nude to conveniently hide the pelvis and breasts. It was a very simple line drawing, unfinished perhaps, but gentle. However, the publication ripped through the community. I wonder about how she shaded the flesh and sketched the flowers. She moved like a ghost through the halls, isolated from most of the others. "They all think I'm weird," she said. Her eyes were the color of tea that had steeped for hours.

My student was, for a while, Chelsea's tragic figure. What can be learned? If she had not published her drawing, I would have no story to tell. And she, perhaps, would not have participated in a special project for the *Boston Globe*. Perhaps she drew from the wound and reached beyond herself. When Boston opened the Sunday paper on February 6, 1994, her self-portrait was there, staring back, the eyes stained but stronger. She has been many different people herself.

With my students' help, I, too, am learning.

Why Teach?

People frequently ask me to tell them stories about moments with my students. I grow tired of such stories. I loathed listening to them around the seminar table in graduate school. My peers had many of these small miracles to relate; my own hands were empty. I walked on no water.

I thought that perhaps I lacked the proper passion to be a teacher. I thought I was too selfish, too focused on silk-spun words, Macbeth's choices, and how to recreate myself each morning without looking back. There is a pain in teaching, a pain that comes whenever a person is forced to consider his or her identity, the origin of all that makes up who we are. There is a pain in confronting the reality that we have very little control, and even more pain in the recognition of how much control we do have. I tell my father, who also teaches, that I lack passion. "What?" he says. "No one can sustain passion. What are you thinking? Commitment, yes. But not passion. Passion isn't really a value. I myself value intimacy. So I find intimacy in teaching. Listen. Roethke wrote that teaching was one of the few professions that allows for love. Understand what you mean when you say passion. You've seen too many westerns."

I watch people's faces on the subway in the morning and think of Ezra Pound's poem about white petals in the dark. I wonder if I am a white petal. My very white hands grip the subway pole as the train lurches to the right, and I recall a line from one of my students. He wrote about his family's move to a new apartment. "We adapted our apartment to our family." I feel my own body giving into the twists and brakes of the train and think about how we people adapt instead—all of us here, our flowering faces glowing in the underground light, our breath and heartbeats indiscernible from the engine's thunder. There is a connection between gripping the subway pole and gripping a piece of chalk. I'm sure of it. The camera is zooming in on my nose.

Reference

Coles, Robert. 1989. *The Call of Stories: Teaching and the Moral Imagination.* Boston: Houghton-Mifflin.

II For the New Teacher

Once we know where we have been, we can plan where we want to go and how to get there. The eleven authors in this section offer both important philosophical and political considerations and specific, practical advice for new teachers. Without glossing over the difficulties and unexpected obstacles, as well as the serendipities, that await the beginning teacher, these authors explore with us some of the ways to sustain our own great beginnings, from seeking out mentors and supportive colleagues, to being alert to the emotional joys and pitfalls of teaching, to staying organized, to finding ways to engage our students as fully as possible in their own learning.

9 New Teachers, Teacher Culture, and School Reform

F. Todd Goodson
East Carolina University

F. Todd Goodson pinpoints one of the most problematic aspects of the new teacher's experience—how to sustain the enthusiasm for innovation and transformation nurtured in the collegial atmosphere of teacher training, once one arrives as a lone newcomer in a school culture that may be resistant to change.

After nine years as a secondary school English teacher, I took a leave, a graduate assistantship, and went back to the university to pursue a doctorate. For my assistantship I taught methods courses and supervised student teachers, but at the same time I took English department seminars filled with doctoral students who were also instructors of freshman composition. I came to understand that the ways in which we induct new instructors into university teaching are very different from the ways we inculturate new secondary teachers, and these differences have important consequences for the emerging professional identities of the new instructors.

New university instructors build their own support communities and pedagogical values within the context of their early teaching experiences and in the company of their peers. Typically, graduate teaching assistants share offices on a different floor, or even building, from full-time, tenure-track faculty. They are crowded together, three or four of them sharing one small office. While these accommodations lack prestige, they afford novice instructors the opportunity to build instructional visions within one another's company. Contrast this situation to what we do to new secondary teachers. They have taken common subject-area and methods courses together at the university, and they might well have begun to develop professional identities and support systems through these experiences. However, at the most crucial point, their actual entry into teaching, we split them apart and drop them (as individuals) into the middle of veteran secondary school faculties.

I believe that this helps to explain one of the most fundamental reasons why we have so much trouble reforming public education. Often, reform comes from younger, or at least newer, members of a community. Certainly, reform will originate with those on the community's periphery, those who have not completely accepted the values at the core of a community's culture. At the university level, graduate assistants sit around and growl about the conservatism of senior professors. But they are doing more than growling; they are building arguments and rationales that, later, they will use to attempt to effect some degree of change. The change will be tempered with experience and according to the situation, but they will have opportunities to push their agendas.

By contrast, novice secondary school teachers (both student teachers and first-year teachers) are routinely faced with discipline problems, a blizzard of official policies and procedures, parental complaints, and the fear that accompanies going in front of a room as The Teacher. For the sake of survival, these new teachers routinely weld themselves to the existing teacher culture. While this does help them survive, any visions for systemic change they might have harbored are typically lost in the process.

This highlights what I believe is the central problem of teacher education—the unsettling gap between the ideals of the university and the practice of the "real world." For example, one day in the methods class we were talking about the teaching of grammar. The class was united in almost evangelical testimony about the sinful nature of teaching grammar in isolation. I left the class to go observe a student teacher (who had taken the course the previous semester) at a local middle school. When I got there, she told me how excited she was that I would be seeing this lesson. She had developed, she told me, a new and exciting approach to the teaching of direct and indirect objects. Essentially, she brought a bag of toys to the class and walked around the room handing them to different students, saying, "I gave the car to John." "I gave the ball to Nancy." "I gave the block to Jennifer." I know that that same student teacher, a few months before, was chanting the grammar-in-isolation-is-bad mantra with the same enthusiasm as the current semester's crop of preservice teachers. After a few weeks in the public school, however, she had forgotten, or, worse yet, had managed through something akin to doublethink, to reconcile her own pedagogical philosophy with that of the existing teacher culture.

As one seasoned instructor of English education once said to me, "It's like the body snatchers get them."

Meanwhile, back at the ivory tower, the graduate assistants have barricaded themselves in their offices and are plotting to include more feminist criticism, or multicultural literature, or gay and lesbian studies, or whatever into the university curriculum. Within certain constraints, they eventually will.

Across campus, in the methods class, students are plotting to include more young adult literature, thematic studies, alternative assessments, or whatever into the public school curriculum. For the most part, they won't.

I believe that the English education community, and schools generally, must begin to more seriously address the way that new teachers are inducted into the profession because I believe that efforts to reform education and the transition of new teachers into teacher culture are inexorably bound together.

Over the past several years, we have witnessed a bewildering assortment of attempts to "reform" schools (e.g., "effective teaching," "effective schools," "America 2000," "mastery learning," "cooperative learning," and on, and on). While there was something of value in each of these reform efforts, I am not satisfied with their progress in changing the ways students and teachers view their work. Each of these reform efforts has originated from outside the public schools; I do not believe that meaningful reform is possible unless it originates with the practitioners. On those occasions where I have felt that I was part of some exciting, innovative approaches in the public schools, it was never the result of directives from principals or district office personnel or state legislators demanding that we do something innovative. Rather, those situations were the result of the right combination of talent and energy working on common problems, and they always involved a degree of tension with the dominant teacher culture. Supervisors of teachers can facilitate reform; they cannot mandate reform. Likewise, while many individual teachers are energetic and creative, teacher culture is a powerful and conservative force that resists change. The dominant teacher culture and the educational status quo are inseparable. Reform must originate with those practitioners who have not fully accepted the values of existing teacher culture.

When I was an undergraduate, our methods instructors told us that we were to be the agents of reform. We were to enter the profession and change it. Sorry. That is too much of a burden to place on the average young person, given the challenges of beginning a teaching career in contemporary public schools; before I could reform schooling, I had to learn to survive within the context of schools. Today, I find myself standing in front of methods classes making ridiculous statements like, "You might never have the opportunity to try the workshop approach, but if you do, say, five or six years from now, these are the sources you should come back to and read." For the most part, students are polite and will dutifully copy things into their notes to make me feel better, but the brutal truth is that the preservice methods class is like trying to teach driver's education without a car. Theory and practice only have meaning in one another's company.

Or, to put all of this in Vygotskyan terms, teachers grow into the profession by acquiring both spontaneous and scientific knowledge. That is, we first attempt to work our way through a task, and, as we develop some experience and competence, we can reflect on the task. It is difficult to reflect meaningfully on a phenomenon (such as teaching) without the context of a base of experience. With at least a rudimentary base of experience, reflection on the task leads back to practice, as we modify, alter, and generally tinker with what we do in attempts to make our practice better.

The tricky thing here is the context in which this takes place. Currently, new teachers gain experience and reflect on this experience within the community of existing teacher culture. To promote meaningful educational reform (and to make, I would hope, the transition into teaching more humane) new voices, attitudes, and support structures need to be made available as a scaffold for the critical early development of new teachers' identities.

Not long ago, I interviewed an experienced high school English teacher (ten years of service). I was looking specifically at the social constraints or boundaries that might act as impediments to teaching and learning in the language arts. The teacher described how, in his *first* year of teaching, parents had complained about the way he taught a required literary masterpiece. Through his words, it is evident that this was a defining event in his professional identity:

> I've been conferenced about the way I approach a lesson, specifically *Hamlet* and the ways in which I have interpreted certain plays in characters' motives, such as the incestuous relationship between Hamlet and his mother. I've been told to tone it down. I was told that it would probably be a good idea to try a more generic approach to the play for the regular classes, while in the honors class, I could go more in depth. I realize that's probably true. . . . She [department chair] had found it successful in a regular class that taking a more generic approach would cause less conflict. After reflection I felt that is basically true. (Goodson 1993, 160–161)

I do not wish to question the professionalism of the department chair in this situation, and I do not mean to suggest that students be forced to study "incest." I am haunted, however, by the resolution of this situation and the enduring effects on the professional identity of this teacher. Clearly, the administrators and department chair were most interested in resolving this situation so as to avoid future conflict. The teacher was told to "tone it down." Most disturbing, the teacher ("after reflection") has adopted the values of his superiors.

No doubt this same teacher, as an undergraduate, was asked to reflect on concepts like censorship, how readers respond to literature, the appropriateness of literary selections for study in high schools, academic freedom, and the like. That reflection was not part of a context of experience. Later, when the teacher did reflect on his experiences, the surrounding context was one that was not terribly interested in heady things like student learning and freedom of speech. Rather, existing school culture tends to view a complaint from any source as a problem that must be eliminated in any manner possible. When we are functioning from within school culture, it is easy to lose sight of the fact that, in resolving conflicts and ensuring that they don't come back, we often throw away some terribly valuable things (e.g., the first amendment, multiple approaches to works of literature, even the works of literature themselves).

It is essential, then, that we be clear about what we mean by "great beginnings" for teachers. There are any number of ways to ease the transition into teacher culture. Many school districts, for example, have established buddy or mentoring systems. These seem very helpful in allowing novices to learn the ropes of a particular school system, but they do this by helping to quickly bond novice teachers to the existing teacher culture. Rather than helping to reform schools, these programs help to resist reform. If we are pleased with the state of public education, then it would be in our interest to help new teachers understand and adapt themselves to existing teacher culture as quickly as possible. If we are not pleased with the public schools, then we need to provide somehow a supportive context where innovative and creative teachers can find the resources and encouragement to initiate reform. I believe that as we look for designs for beginning teachers, we must provide somehow for those new teachers to be able to hear and see the value in alternatives to the practices and standards of current teacher and school culture.

References

Goodson, F. Todd. 1993. Defining Community: The High School as Rhetorical Situation. Ph.D. Diss. University of Kansas.

Vygotsky, Lev S. 1962. *Thought and Language*. Edited and translated by Eugenia Hanfmann and Gertrude Vakar. Cambridge, MA: MIT Press.

———. 1978. *Mind in Society*. Cambridge, MA: Harvard University Press.

10 Gone but Not Forgotten: University-Based Support for Beginning Teachers

Mary C. McMackin
Lesley College

Judith A. Boccia
University of Massachusetts–Lowell

Mary C. McMackin and Judith A. Boccia examine low retention rates among new teachers and describe the unique program Chalktalk, a collaborative effort among new teachers, veteran teachers, and university faculty, implemented by the University of Massachusetts–Lowell, that meets the specific needs of novice teachers, motivating them to continue in the profession.

Teacher retention is a major concern in many of our schools. As many as 30 percent of our beginning teachers leave the profession by the end of their second year, with up to 50 percent leaving by the end of five years (Colbert and Wolff 1992; Heyns 1988; Schlechty and Vance 1981).

What Factors Contribute to This High Attrition Rate?

Chapman (1984) believes that genetic factors, learning experiences, performance skills, environmental conditions, and cognitive/emotional responses all impact the beginning teacher's decision to either remain in the profession or leave. Veenman (1984) attributes the difficulties that many beginning teachers experience to a phenomenon he calls "reality shock." Veenman (1984) points out that, "In general, this concept ["reality shock"] is used to indicate the collapse of the missionary ideals formed during teacher training by the harsh and rude reality of everyday classroom life" (143). The beginning teacher, addressing this reality every day, is often faced with a unique set of external and internal pressures that can become overwhelming. These pressures may arise from personal ideals and philosophies that are in direct conflict with the existing educational environment.

In seeking to assimilate a balance between their ideals and reality, many beginning teachers may experience the following indications of "reality shock" (Müller-Fohrbrodt, Cloetta, and Dann 1978 as cited in Veenman 1984):

- complaints about work load and personal health (physical and emotional);
- changes in teaching behavior and style;
- changes in attitudes that point to a shift away from initial philosophies and ideals;
- changes in personality, which may be reflected in a poor self-concept and weakened self-image; and
- a desire to leave the profession prematurely.

This "reality shock" may be intensified by the beginning teacher's feelings of loneliness and detachment, for isolation is often endemic to teaching (Gehrke 1991). This is particularly true for beginning teachers who may be the only novice in the school or system. Evans (1989) points out that "75 percent [of teachers in the teaching force] have been teaching for at least 10 years; 50 percent, for 15 years or more" (10).

In order for beginning teachers to rise above the negative influences that can lead to attrition and to successfully survive their induction years, collaborative support from within the educational community must be forthcoming.

What Can Be Done to Help Beginning Teachers Survive Induction?

Chapman (1984) found that the quality of the beginning teacher's first professional experience was a stronger indicator of retention than was either the teacher's academic ability or the quality of the program that prepared the teacher for this career. Yet, many beginning teachers enter their first assignment faced with two choices: sink or swim.

Boccia (1992) found that only 17 percent of 115 beginning teachers surveyed were offered orientation programs designed exclusively for beginning teachers. Because teachers are faced with myriad decisions each day, it is not surprising that 89 percent of these beginning teachers sought out the assistance of a veteran colleague to help them during their induction years (i.e., the first three years in the profession).

When questioned as to the type of assistance these same beginning teachers would find most helpful, they responded by placing the following three choices at the top of their "wish list": an opportunity to share experiences with other beginning teachers (66 percent), an opportunity to observe other classes (66 percent), and workshops designed specifically for beginning teachers (65 percent) (Boccia 1992, 9).

On the basis of beginning teacher research (such as Odell and Ferraro 1992; Veenman 1984) and especially the research of Boccia (1988; 1990), the University of Massachusetts–Lowell implemented Chalktalk, a support network designed to meet the specific needs of novice teachers.

In order to foster a collaborative effort among beginning teachers, veteran teachers, and university faculty, an advisory board of about ten highly regarded veteran teachers was convened the year Chalktalk was first implemented. Today, these teachers continue to meet regularly to plan bimonthly workshops at the university. Although the agendas for these workshops are planned by the members of the advisory board, the *topics* for the workshops are always chosen by the beginning teachers. The topics included

- Classroom management
- How to maintain creativity
- Record-keeping and organizational skills
- Ending the year: Making May and June less hectic

Other topics have included

- Parental concerns/parent conferences
- School law

At the close of each workshop, a questionnaire is distributed. Each participant is asked to (1) select a topic for the next workshop, (2) indicate what aspect(s) of the current workshop were useful, and (3) suggest ways to improve the workshop(s).

Invariably, the beginning teachers have responded that they enjoy exchanging "war stories" with peers, and that they have benefited from the suggestions and advice of the veteran teachers, who act as facilitators and coaches during the workshops. The novice teachers have consistently pointed out that they value the opportunity to talk about their failings and frustrations with colleagues *from outside* their own system.

In the Chalktalk model, new teachers are not paired with designated mentors; rather, they are free to sit and discuss their concerns with peers and veterans who share common philosophies and teaching styles. Allowing the beginning teachers the opportunity to choose a compatible source of support is an important factor in the Chalktalk model, for unless an appropriate rapport is established between the novice and veteran, insurmountable limitations may be placed on the relationship and little, if any, support may be forthcoming. Additionally, since the veteran teachers play no role in evaluating the performance of the beginning teachers, the novices usually feel very comfortable seeking support and advice.

How Do Beginning Teachers Benefit from Chalktalk?

Induction is a complex, multiyear process. "If we want to retain new teachers, particularly those teaching in inner-city schools, we must introduce them to the profession humanely, in ways that engender self-esteem, competence, collegiality, and professional stature" (Colbert and Wolff, 1992, 193).

Two objectives of Chalktalk have been (1) to address the common professional concerns of first-, second-, and third-year teachers through bimonthly seminars, and (2) to link the university with veteran and novice teachers. These objectives are met as the beginning teachers

- share experiences and ideas with other beginning teachers;
- receive support, advice, and suggestions from a team of veteran teachers;
- find answers to specific problems they face on a daily basis;
- extend their knowledge base through the distribution of professional materials;
- engage with experts in related fields; and
- develop skills and adapt strategies that enhance their teaching.

According to Jacullo-Noto (1986), in order for teachers to maintain a positive attitude about their job, 3R's are essential: respect, recognition, and reinforcement. Chalktalk continually strives to maintain an atmosphere based on these 3R's. For example, to acknowledge the respect and recognition of teachers as professionals, refreshments are served at each planning session and workshop, computer-printed name tags are prepared bimonthly for Chalktalk participants, and all participants are encouraged to take part in the topic selection and evaluation of the workshops. Furthermore, to provide reinforcement for new skills and strategies, presentations are given by guest speakers, individual binders containing pertinent articles and ideas are provided at each workshop, and probably most important, collaborative problem solving exists within a safe environment.

What Impact Has Chalktalk Had on Veteran Teachers?

The zeal with which the Chalktalk advisory board members have responded to this support network has been truly amazing. The veterans seem to value these experiences with their colleagues as much as, if not more than, do the beginning teachers. Research in the field of adult learning supports a rationale for the excitement demonstrated by the veterans.

Krupp (1989), in her description of the developmental stages of adult learners, points out that, generally speaking, people in their twenties ask two questions—"Can I?" and "How do I?"—while people in their thirties, forties, and fifties seek to share their ideas with others and often aspire to leadership roles. Through Chalktalk, each age group seems to find links that promote level-appropriate personal and professional development.

Morimoto, Gregory, and Butler (1973) state that people begin to make meaning when they are heard. For many of the veteran teachers, Chalktalk provides a unique medium through which they can voice their ideas and thus expand their own capacity for meaning. Furthermore, Chalktalk affords veteran teachers opportunities to reflect on their own educational philosophies and reaffirm their own beliefs.

Finally, Chalktalk fosters social interaction for teachers, a component that is often overlooked in daily teaching and learning. Thus, Chalktalk appears to have been at least partially responsible for affecting opportunities to

- engender a renewed enthusiasm for teaching among the veterans;
- provide the experienced teachers with a means of evaluating and reaffirming their own educational philosophy; and
- extend the professional development of the veteran teachers to a unique level.

Although Chalktalk has not solved all the problems that novice teachers face as they move from being full-time students to full-time professionals, it does serve as a model of collaborative support that meets the specific needs of this particular community of teachers. The goal of Chalktalk is to provide a context for assistance that allows each new teacher (1) to experience a successful entry into the profession and (2) to continue to grow both personally and professionally. The value of this program will be measured by its impact on the teachers it serves (both novice and veteran) and the students they serve throughout their careers.

References

Boccia, Judith A. 1988. *Chalktalk: A Study of Professional Concerns in the First Three Years of Teaching. Part I: Secondary Teachers.* Lowell, MA: University of Massachusetts Lowell, Center for Field Services and Studies.

———. 1990. *Chalktalk: A Study of Professional Concerns in the First Three Years of Teaching. Part II: Elementary Teachers.* Lowell, MA: University of Massachusetts Lowell, Center for Field Services and Studies.

———. 1992. *Chalktalk: Professional Concerns in the First Three Years of Teaching.* Lowell: University of Massachusetts Lowell, Center for Field Services and Studies.

Chapman, D. W. 1984. "Teacher Retention: The Test of a Model." *American Educational Research Journal* 21.3: 645–58.

Colbert, J. A. and D. E. Wolff. 1992. "Surviving in Urban Schools: A Collaborative Model for a Beginning Teacher Support System." *Journal of Teacher Education* 43.3: 193–99.

Evans, R. 1989. "The Faculty in Midcareer: Implications for School Improvement." *Educational Leadership* 46.8: 10–15.

Gehrke, Nathalie J. 1991. "Seeing Our Way to Better Helping of Beginning Teachers." *Educational Forum* 55.3: 233–42.

Heyns, B. 1988. "Educational Defectors: A First Look at Teacher Attrition in the NLS-72." *Educational Researcher* 17.3: 24–32.

Jacullo-Noto, J. 1986. "Interactive Research and Development: Partners in Craft." In *Rethinking School Improvement: Research, Craft and Concept,* ed. Ann Lieberman. New York: Teachers College Press, 176–90.

Krupp, J. A. 1989. "Staff Development and the Individual." *Staff Development: A Handbook of Effective Practices,* ed. Sarah DeJarnette Caldwell. Oxford, OH: National Staff Development Council, 44–56.

Morimoto, K., J. Gregory and P. Butler. 1973. "Context for Learning." *Harvard Educational Review* 43.2: 245–57.

Müller-Fohrbrodt, G., B. Cloetta, and H. D. Dann. 1978. *Der Praxisschock bei junger Lehrern.* Stuttgart: Klett.

Odell, S. J. and D. P. Ferraro. 1992. "Teacher Mentoring and Teacher Retention." *Journal of Teacher Education* 43.3: 200–4.

Schlechty, P. C. and V. S. Vance. 1981. "Do Academically Able Teachers Leave Education? The North Carolina Case." *Phi Delta Kappan* 63: 106–12.

Veenman, Simon. 1984. "Perceived Problems of Beginning Teachers." *Review of Educational Research* 54.2: 143–78.

11 Avoiding Burn-out: New Teachers Dialoguing with Experienced Teachers

Regina Paxton Foehr
Illinois State University

Regina Paxton Foehr looks at the serious stress that drives up to half of new teachers out of the profession within five years, and finds one solution in a dialogue between student and experienced teachers that generated a list of helpful tips, and, more important, a feeling of support and collaboration.

I will never forget the telephone call I received from a student teacher and her sheepish voice at the end of her first day of student teaching, its strain giving away her struggle to fight back tears. Trying to sound lighthearted, she stammered out the words:

> You'll never believe what happened on my first day of teaching. A fist fight broke out in my class, and one boy was hospitalized with a broken nose.

She had wanted to be the first to tell me, her university English supervisor. Rumors of the fight had spread quickly throughout the large school, and the (Thumbs up) "Go get 'em Teach" remarks and good-natured smiles of other teachers in the hallway that day had helped only a little to offset the humiliation she felt at such public embarrassment.

Such situations can be the worst nightmares-come-true of any teacher, especially student teachers and new, nontenured teachers whose reputations in the profession have not been established and whose future employability, they fear, hinges upon their ability to uphold professional standards in their teaching and in the atmosphere of their classrooms. They have deep concerns about job security and survival, especially in areas where enrollments are declining. Moreover, among new teachers in particular, the stress of such situations can lead quickly to fractured self-esteem, burn-out, and the decision to leave the profession. The stress is so great for newly trained teachers, in fact, that one-third to one-half of all new teachers leave the profession within their first five years of teaching (Darling-Hammond 1990, 5).

With the demands of day-to-day "teaching," the idealism of new teachers can easily get lost in the reality of responsibilities. Despite an initial love for literature and writing and a desire to instill that love in their students, new teachers sometimes find just getting through the day to be their goal. At a seminar for student teachers who were returning to the Illinois State University (ISU) campus midway through the experience, one student teacher shared her discouragement:

> When some of my students are getting high on crack between classes, it's hard to even think about putting into practice all the things we learned in our methods classes.

Another said,

> I'm student teaching in a small rural school where you'd think it would be safe, but we just had a faculty meeting on gangs, and two gang recruiters are in my classes and I'm scared.

As twenty-five-year-old teacher, Ann Marie Radaskiewicz Butson writes:

> I became a teacher because I was anxious to share my love of language and literature with young people. But at the end of the day . . . I wonder if I [have] influenced even one of my 130 students today. I was a janitor, a psychologist, a security officer, a secretary, and a social worker. But was I a teacher? The sun sets on another day of frustration and disillusionment. And I have to do it again tomorrow. (Butson 1989, 8)

Most student teachers have high expectations of themselves and believe that they will be able to motivate their students to enjoy learning. But often they discover that instead of being an inspiration, they may be perceived by students as an adversary or an unwanted intrusion. At the end of what she described as a successful student teaching experience, one student teacher contrasted the dream and the reality of the experience:

> My eyes were opened. The dream is that your students will be raising their hands and doing their homework *for you,* but the reality is maybe one person raises their hands or does their homework. The reality is that they say, "This is dumb. This is stupid. . . ." It's hard work when the kids think you're a dork.

In addition, disillusionment may occur in other areas. For example, instead of the expected support and mentoring among faculty, new teachers may experience disappointment over not having their needs taken into account by other faculty members. One first-year teacher said,

> You're low man on the totem pole; all the other teachers have snagged all the new teachers' editions, staplers, and supplies. I'm not kidding—you're the new teacher, the one who needs the teacher's edition, but you're low man on the totem pole—that I find disturbing.

While crisis situations, fear, disillusionment, and burn-out can happen to any teacher, new teachers are particularly vulnerable. I believe, however, that in many cases, crisis and disillusionment could be offset, or even avoided altogether, if teachers entered their class-rooms with access to the wisdom earned through the experience of others in the profession. Whether dealing with student behavior, learning, or other issues important to teaching, those in the profession who are actively teaching usually have the experience to anticipate problems before they arise because they have encountered them pre-viously. Surveys tell us that both first-year and experienced teachers recognize this. They rank direct and immediate access to advice and assistance as most helpful in becoming a more effective teacher (*Metropolitan Life Survey of the American Teacher* 1991a, 1991b).

Ironically, however, whether in rural or urban, private or public, large or small schools, new and inexperienced teachers do not always have access to experienced teachers who are willing to help or the con-fidence to approach the experienced teachers they do know. As one new English teacher in a small-town school confided to me,

> I feel as if I was misled during the job interview when all the teachers seemed to work together and care about each other. Now that I'm here, I see that they all just shut their doors and stick to themselves. I feel so lonely.

One reason teachers burn out is that they are burning alone (Berthoff 1990, 368). For new teachers or student teachers, their own vulnerability, their insecurity in their lack of experience, and their fear of looking foolish—or worse, incompetent—can make tapping into the knowledge and experience of other teachers difficult. In particular, early in their teaching experience, when they most need the help of oth-ers, many new teachers are so intimidated by experienced teachers that they choose not to intrude on their time by asking them questions. In addition, new teachers are often afraid to admit "weakness" to build-ing administrators who have the responsibility of evaluating them.

The Harvard University School of Education recognizes the isolation and vulnerability that new teachers feel. In "First Aid for First-Year Teachers," Katherine K. Merseth (1992) discusses an electronic computer network available nationwide to graduates of Harvard University's teacher education programs who are in their first year of teaching. This computer network, available through Harvard's School of Education, is set up to support and encourage these first-year teachers. The network links them with each other as well as Harvard faculty and staff, a small number of invited second-year teachers, and other invited guests (679).

This type of network seems to be an ideal way to engage teachers in collaborative mentoring, stress reduction, and problem-solving dialogues. Most new teachers, however, do not have access to such an electronic mail system.

Collaboration as a Solution

I believe, however, that we need also to promote a spirit of collaboration among teachers, preteachers, and student teachers and to encourage them to share and take advantage of one another's knowledge and experience. At ISU, twice during student teaching, our student teachers return to campus to dialogue about their experiences and to offer support, encouragement, and possible solutions to problems. To engage prestudent teachers in such dialogues, I have asked those in my methods classes, "The Teaching of Writing," to interview experienced teachers from English and other disciplines to discover and record their advice and suggestions on not just how to survive the student teaching experience, but how to succeed as teachers themselves.

Much to their surprise, after they conducted these interviews, the student teachers reported that the experienced teachers were eager to express their views and were genuinely interested in helping them. I believe that their dialogue provided an important collaborative experience in two areas: (1) in opening up communication within and across disciplines and student/teacher ranks and (2) in producing new and useful knowledge as the preteachers created and shared the results of their interviews with the class. The experience of interviewing gave these prestudent teachers a feeling of being members of the profession and an experience of collegiality with their soon-to-be colleagues and mentors. It also gave them an indication of what other teachers consider important in teaching, and it let them know that problems can arise even for experienced teachers.

Participants in the Dialogues

The semester before they began student teaching, thirty students, all senior English education majors, participated in the assignment, each of them conducting informal interviews with from one to four teachers. The approximately ninety participating teachers taught in schools from Central to Northern Illinois, representing large and small, rural, urban, and inner-city schools. Students were told to write down the teachers' suggestions but to weigh their value for themselves as to whether each suggestion should be taken. After reading the teachers' suggestions, I found that their suggestions could be organized and listed under seven main categories: *Be Professional, Be Prepared, Be Organized, Be Patient, Be a Real Person and Honor Each Student as a Real Person, Be Sensible with Discipline,* and *Be Aware of Your Own Needs.* A copy of the resulting list (see below) was issued to each of the students before each began student teaching.[1] All tips that students submitted to me were included on the list; when tips were given by more than one teacher, however, they were recorded only once.

Tips for the Beginning Teacher

I. Be Professional

1. Be professional in dress, manner, and attitude from the first minute that you are present in the classroom.
2. Act professionally in public.
3. Use language appropriately. Don't resort to using slang too often.
4. Speak clearly and loudly enough to be heard.
5. Don't be late to class.
6. Don't come late to staff meetings.
7. When dealing with confrontation, maintain your composure.
8. Know when to compromise.
9. State your opinion—let others know where you stand.
10. Have a positive attitude.
11. Establish a good rapport with parents and administration.
12. Keep good, strong lines of communication open between you and the parents.
13. Don't be afraid to call parents if one of your students is having problems in class. Many parents have no idea how well their children are doing in school until report card time rolls around, so they will appreciate your efforts to keep them informed.

14. Don't be afraid to call or meet with parents. They are probably just as curious about you as you are about them. In fact, knowing them might help you to better understand their child.

15. Call or write parents when their son or daughter does something good or improves in class. Don't limit communication to bad news.

16. Encourage parents to be proud of their children.

17. Show students that you care about their lives, and show the parents that you care about their children's progress.

18. When conducting parent-teacher conferences, have handouts ready for the parents that include your philosophy, your grading policy, your attendance policies, and their child's grades.

19. Get to know the principal of your school. Invite the principal to sit in on your class when he or she has a chance and ask for any suggestions that might improve your teaching. Good rapport with the administration is invaluable.

20. Ask other teachers, even the principal, for advice.

21. Use discretion in deciding which teachers to approach for information. Don't be suspicious—be observant and selective.

22. Show respect to the cooperating teacher and the other faculty.

23. Cooperate with your colleagues, be willing to ask them for help, and be open to offering your advice.

24. Get to know the custodian and the secretary.

25. Ask for a student handbook and a teacher's handbook. Be familiar with administrative expectations and procedures.

26. Familiarize yourself with departmental policies.

27. Read the latest research manuals in your field.

28. Attend workshops regularly.

29. Know your rights as a teacher (union contracts/district rules).

30. Know the resources or how to make proper referrals for special education, discipline, etc.

31. When conferencing with students in a private office, always leave the door open.

32. Never touch your students.

33. Remember that the way you solve problems will become a model for your students when they encounter problems.

34. Never share really personal information with your students. It is important to maintain a teacher-student relationship with them.

35. Devise a detailed rationale. Know and explain why your students should meet your objectives.

II. Be Prepared

1. Do not wait until the last minute to devise unit or lesson plans. Take time to research your ideas before you try them out.

2. Have daily lesson plans well prepared.

3. Always plan more for each class period than you think you can accomplish.

4. Have lesson plans ready for substitute teachers.

5. Have extra activities for students to do in that "left over" time at the end of the hour.

6. Don't expect every class to react the same to various activities and discussions.

7. Always have examples ready that are relevant to the students' lives.

8. Always have an alternate explanation.

9. Be flexible.

10. Don't ever throw anything away.

11. Know how to use equipment such as the VCR and television. Nothing is more embarrassing than ruining such a machine in front of twenty pairs of eyes.

12. Be self-confident. Be able to explain the importance of your curriculum or why the student received the grade he or she did.

13. Know where the fire exits are located. Be familiar with disaster procedures. Be prepared!

III. Be Organized

1. It is important to feel prepared as well as look prepared.

2. Thoroughly prepare lecture notes, mini-lessons, questions for discussion, and class activities each day.

3. If you expect your students to have all of their materials, then your should have yours, too.

4. Clearly state objectives and exactly what you expect on assignments—students need a picture sometimes.

5. The students always want to know what is due and when. Write assignments on the board daily and verbally remind them of due dates.

6. Give students plenty of advance warning regarding assignment due dates, and give students a copy of the syllabus early in the semester. It is also a good idea to mail a copy of the syllabus home to students' parents.

7. Set grading criteria for letter grades on all tests and essays before giving them to the students.

8. When grading students' writing assignments, give them a cover sheet with a checklist. Check any mechanical or organizational mistakes the students make on the checklist. This way, the students know exactly why they received the grade they did.

9. To save time and prevent confusion, before handing back student papers, tests, and homework, categorize them by seating arrangement or alphabetize them.

10. In order to avoid the "who-needs-what-paper" dilemma because he or she was absent, keep a file. If a student is absent, put the student's name on the top of the handout, and keep it for when the student returns.

11. Have students take responsibility for their absent peers. They can collect handouts and assignments and put them in a folder designed for that purpose.

12. Acquire a school calendar so that you'll know when students have days off and when other important activities are scheduled.

13. Keep a schedule of each class in a plastic cover. If you give a student permission to leave for the library, restroom, or somewhere else, use a dry erase marker to indicate on the plastic cover where the student has gone.

14. Keep manuals in one place.

15. Keep your desk and files organized.

16. Keep two folders for student work for each period you teach, one for papers you have graded and one for papers you haven't graded yet. This is especially helpful if your students are turning in a lot of papers each week.

17. Be sure to have a record of lesson plans.

18. A good way to organize the material you collect is to keep binders for each teaching unit.

19. Try to keep track of the books you loan out. Using note cards for each book, write the names of the students who check out your books, and keep a book file.

IV. Be Patient

1. Give students enough thinking time.

2. Don't tell your students the answer simply because a few seconds have passed in silence. Wait longer, minutes even, before restating the question, but don't answer it yourself.

3. If students don't respond to a question right away, or if they express confusion, ask lead-in questions.

4. Remember that students will be absent, so don't get too frustrated when having to reschedule assignments and activities.

5. Realize and accept that not all students will remain at the same level academically.

6. Listen attentively to students' problems.

V. Be a Real Person, and Honor Each Student as a Real Person

1. Treat your students with respect at all times. Never embarrass a student or make a student feel bad about himself or herself.

2. Never use sarcasm toward your students.

3. Be firm, but be flexible, when it's needed.

4. Don't dislike any student—dislike behaviors or attitudes.

5. Make an effort to include all students.

6. Keep prejudice out of the classroom.

7. Encourage leadership and confidence in all students.

8. Encourage students to dream.

9. Recognize students who do outstanding work as well as those who need to improve.

10. Always let students know when they have done a good job.

11. Don't be an enforcer or know-it-all. Let the students see the real you.

12. Do not pretend to be all-knowing—we all learn together.

13. Admit when you are wrong.

14. If you make a mistake, don't give up. Keep trying until you get it right. It is OK for a student to see a teacher mess up—this makes teachers seem more like real people.

15. Do not be unapproachable.

16. Do not follow the "Never Smile before Thanksgiving" rule.

17. Smile. Enthusiasm is an important ingredient for a good learning environment.

18. Maintain a sense of humor with students.

19. Know students as well as you can. Know their strengths and weaknesses.

20. Know the students' names. This will help establish a good rapport with them.

21. Be a good listener.

22. Let students know that if they have a problem, they can share it in confidence with you.

23. Let your students know that you enjoy your job and that you want to be with them.

VI. Be Sensible with Discipline

1. Establish firm ground rules regarding class conduct on the first day of class and stick to those rules. Having a firm discipline policy laid out at the beginning of the school year is essential for new teachers.

2. Always make clear to students what you expect and follow through.

3. Know the school's discipline policy and adhere to it.

4. Always document discipline problems, especially recurring ones. You may need this documentation when talking to parents or administrators.

5. Don't be afraid to talk to fellow teachers about problems you are having or to the school counselors—that's what they are there for.

6. Be sure to let parents know early if there is a problem.

7. Don't let problems occur more than three times without doing something about them. If necessary, take students out into the hall and discuss problems there or ask the student to stay after school to work out problems.

8. Avoid confrontations in the classroom at all costs!

9. Do not argue with a student during class. Discuss the problem one-on-one after class.

10. Have solid rules and procedures for discipline. Do not send every discipline problem to the principal because it will show that you cannot handle your class. Keep the discipline and the students inside of the classroom.

11. Do not be too strict in class. Do not yell or reprimand students each time they talk out of turn or break the silence. Give students some freedom.

12. In disciplining, don't approach students from an adversarial standpoint. Let them know that the rules are designed to provide guidance so that everyone has the opportunity to achieve without any interference from others.

13. Let students know that you have confidence in them, and that you have set high expectations for their achievement. Affirm positive behavior and achievement.

14. Be consistent in the way you deal with students; don't offer special treatment or excessive punishment to anyone, ever.

15. Respond fairly and wisely.

16. Give the students the benefit of the doubt.

17. If a student is acting up, try standing near the student and make clear eye contact with him or her. Giving the student a stern look works well too.

18. Walk around the class. Move about through their desks and make your presence known. This increases attention.

19. Do not judge your students by your own personal standards.

20. Make the rules and punishments reasonable.

21. Be authoritative, not authoritarian.

22. Set the tone for the day if you go on a field trip. Discreetly let students know that you are still the authority, even though you are in a different environment from that of the school.

23. "Never let them see you sweat." If they know they can walk all over you, they will.

VII. Be Aware of Your Own Needs

1. Give yourself relaxation or "self" time every day, even if it is only thirty minutes.

2. Take time out to deal with stress when it does happen.

3. Don't take on more activities than you can handle. Learn to say, "No!"

4. Try to get enough sleep and exercise.

5. Inform your significant others that you will be busy.

6. Read and write for yourself.

7. Strive for excellence, not perfection.

8. Respect yourself. Respect for others will follow.

As the class discussed the teachers' suggestions, students frequently expressed appreciation for a suggestion that they themselves had not previously considered. In some cases student teachers shared the lists with their cooperating teachers. The teachers seemed to appreciate that our students were getting some practical suggestions from experienced teachers, in addition to the theoretical and pedagogical knowledge from their coursework. In at least one case, after a cooperating teacher showed a high school administrator the list of suggestions, that administrator, who was from a school of about 2,000 students, made copies of the suggestions to give to new teachers at his school. Thus the interview assignment became the impetus for dialogue to take place at many levels: student teacher to student teacher, student teacher to teacher, teacher to administrator, and administrator to new teacher.

I believe that this activity helped the prestudent teachers in several ways. It engaged them in considering and confronting issues that they might otherwise not have considered before they entered the profession. Such consideration and confrontation can serve as "an ounce of prevention" instead of the usually painful "pound of cure." The activity also engaged them in meaningful dialogue with other professionals on issues important to the student teachers. These dialogues would probably not have taken place except among the most outgoing of student teachers, if the student teachers themselves had not been assigned to interview experienced teachers. The dialogues became a way for student teachers to recognize, hear, and honor their own and each other's voices. It allowed the students to produce collaboratively, as part of an academic group, what was for them new knowledge. And finally, the list they created then served as a text for their current and future reference, to remind the student teachers of ways to navigate the teaching experience as they began what can, at times, be a daunting experience even under the best of circumstances.

Note

1. Thanks to the efforts of Deborah Loest, then a student in the class but now a first-year teacher at Morton Junior High School, Morton, Illinois, the list was typed in time for student teaching.

References

Berthoff, Ann. 1990. "Paulo Freire's Liberation Pedagogy." *Language Arts* 67.4 (April): 362–69.

Butson, Ann Marie Radaskiewicz. 1989. "Inside the Classroom." *Newsweek* 113 (5 June): 8.

Darling-Hammond, Linda. 1990. *Teacher Supply, Demand, and Quality.* Washington, DC: National Board for Professional Teaching Standards, 5.

Merseth, Katherine K. 1992. "First Aid for First-Year Teachers." *Phi Delta Kappan* 73.9 (May): 678–83.

Metropolitan Life Survey of the American Teacher, 1991: Coming to Terms— Teachers' Views on Current Issues in Education. 1991a. New York: Metropolitan Life Insurance Company.

Metropolitan Life Survey of the American Teacher, 1991: The First Year—New Teachers' Expectations and Ideals. 1991b. New York: Metropolitan Life Insurance Company.

12 What I Know Now: The Personal and the Emotional in Teaching English

Paul Heilker
Virginia Polytechnic Institute and State University

Paul Heilker explores what he has found to be the "single most important" aspect of teaching, yet ironically the one he was least prepared for: how our feelings (both positive and negative) toward our students, our own personal lives, and our students' need for emotional support affect our teaching.

As I worked my way through the training program that certified me to teach secondary school in New York some years ago, I studied quite a bit about the various philosophies of education, theories and taxonomies of students' cognitive and moral development, behavioral objectives, methods of instruction, learning styles and learning disabilities, options for evaluation, procedures for constructing testing mechanisms, techniques for maintaining authority and order, theories of reading and writing, theories of adolescent psychology, and the like. Thus, I thought I was thoroughly prepared to move into my first teaching assignment: five sections of ninth-grade English. I was most mistaken.

What I was thoroughly *unprepared* for, what I found to be the most difficult and taxing part of my new job, what we did *not* study in my certification program, was just how personal and emotional teaching is. Looking back, I realize that my study of abstract theories about an absurdly overgeneralized conceptual category—"students"—did nothing to prepare me for the exhausting emotional work and the disconcerting but inevitable clashes between my personal and professional lives that teaching entails. If I had known then what I know now, my entry into teaching would have been less traumatic. At the end of my first term of teaching, I was tired—physically, mentally, and spiritually tired. But most of all, having had no previous warning or inkling of any kind about just how personal and emotional teaching is, at the end of my first term of teaching I was emotionally wiped out, drained, exhausted, empty.

I'm not sure why we don't discuss the personal and emotional nature of teaching in our training programs, but I think it has to do with maintaining the appearance of some kind of masculine, objective "seriousness" in these programs. I think we avoid discussing the personal and the emotional in teaching in order to show that we are worshiping the correct scholarly gods of "rigor" and "logic." Or perhaps we don't want to sully the pure pursuit of abstract knowledge with the messy complications of real life: real, whole students with real, whole lives and real, whole problems. Regardless of the cause, I wish to address this lack. I want to discuss this unfortunately and unnecessarily taboo topic and help prepare new teachers for the personal and the emotional aspects of their careers, a preparation I did not have and which cost me dearly. I want beginning teachers to know now what I didn't know then. Here's some of what I've learned:

■ People who are new to the profession and struggling to develop as teachers are often paralyzed by their dysfunctional relationships with their students on a personal level. My friend Stephanie, for instance, said recently, "I know it's wrong, and I wish I didn't feel this way, but I just don't like my students very much." Or worse yet was Sue's case last year. "My students hate me," she told me dejectedly, "I know it." Never, in all my training as a teacher or in my seven years of teaching, has anyone ever mentioned to me that I might not like my students or that they might hate me. No one has ever told me whether such a situation was common, or OK, or even forgivable. No one has ever told me to be prepared for such a possibility or what I might do about it if it arose. And it does arise. My functioning as a teacher has been repeatedly disrupted by the frustration, anger, resentment, and even rage I have felt toward particular students. But we don't talk about that.

■ There comes a time each semester when I have to tell my students that I am a hard grader and that I criticize their papers in depth and detail, not because I hate them, but because I like them very much. They sometimes have trouble understanding that. Furthermore, I have to repeatedly reassure them that when I am evaluating their work, their grades are not based on how much I like or dislike them on a personal basis, but on how effective their writing is. Students have a very difficult time separating criticism of their work from criticism of them personally. So do I, of course. It is, in fact, impossible to separate the two. When you criticize the written text I have produced, you are criticizing the text from which it originated, the text of my self. So when I tell a concerned student, "There's nothing personal meant by this F," I am lying both to that student and to myself. It's *very* personal. What that letter F is saying is that I do not like the self that produced this text and that I want you to know it and to change into someone I can like better. I also have a little speech—it has become almost automatic—that runs like this: "Your grades are not determined by how much I like you as a person. I have often had to give A's to people I despise and to give D's to people I really like." But that is not the whole truth, of course. If I have students on the dividing line between a B and a C, and I have no objective factors with which to push them one way or another over the split, I rely on a simple formula: How much do I like them? A strong feeling one way or the other usually decides the matter.

■ I realize now that I want my students to like me, and it hurts when they don't. I *do* things so that they *will* like me—pump up grades, give them second chances, let them out early, use audiovisual equipment in class, downplay the importance of grammar and mechanics, tell jokes, act like a clown, and so on.

■ As I think about it, in my own experience, I have been motivated to work for those instructors I liked, even when I hated the material; and I have loathed working for those I didn't like, even when I loved the subject matter. I was glad to take low grades from teachers I despised. And, most interesting, it seems, the grades I received from the teachers I liked were (and still are) far less important than the sense that they liked me back. That sense that they liked me back, *that* was my motivation and my reward.

■ I love my students. I mean that. I love them. I love them like a parent or an older sibling. "Take care of your health," I tell them. "Eat well. Get your sleep. If you get a cough, for goodness sake, go to the health center. There are more important things than grades, like your mental and emotional stability, for instance. Geez! Wear socks, Julie! It's thirty-eight degrees outside! How many of you are feeling a little depressed? Frantic? Well, it's November slump time. Students just like you across the country are just as tired, just as frightened by how little time is left in the semester and how much work they have to do, just as saddened by the coming of winter. You are not alone. Take care of yourselves over break. Drive carefully. Don't drink and drive." And just before Spring Break, I always find myself acting as older brother, warning the young women that, as every "Oprah" show attests, guys are slime.

■ I love my students. I feel close to them. I want them to know that, too. So, I often find myself having to pull back from the impulse to touch them physically, restraining myself from patting them on the back, from touching their arms as I look over their shoulders at what they are writing. There is always the fear that such a touch will be misconstrued. And there is always the danger of that feeling of closeness and that desire to touch turning into something else, proceeding either from my students or from me, I'm afraid to say. But I have to say it. I cannot forget, though we seldom talk about it, that teachers and students do become romantically involved. No one ever told me that I might become romantically (if not sexually) attracted to some of my students. No one ever told me to beware of this possibility or what I might do to avoid it or to deal with it if it *did* happen. No one ever told me that there are relationships, romantic and otherwise, between teachers and students that are not imaginary, or mutual, or reciprocal, or consensual, or appreciated, that sexual harassment *is* a reality in student-teacher relationships, or that the violations can go even further. I know teachers who live in fear of being seriously hurt, if not killed, by their students. And a good friend of mine was raped by one of her teachers.

■ In *my* teaching, I project a parental kind of love, I suppose. I hope. And it is usually as a parent that I am invoked. For instance, the other day, as I was walking into class, my student Anna stopped me and said, while pointing to a young man I can only assume is her boyfriend, "Mr. Heilker, make him stop smoking. It's driving me *crazy!*" "Smoking *is* stupid," I said, "but I can't make him stop. All I can do is make him stop smoking in this building, since it's against the rules. So take it outside, pal." But even as I was saying this, in my mind, I heard distinct echoes from my own childhood: "Dad, Karen won't stay on her side of the car. And she keeps *touching* me. Make her stop!"

■ As I think about it, I was unprepared for the emotional demands of this parental role when I began teaching. Indeed, I was not aware of or prepared for the emotional demands of any of the roles I was most frequently called upon to enact in my new position: parent, older sibling, best friend, confidant, confessor, disciplinarian, bully, psychotherapist, arbitrator, and so on. My role as *teacher*, I now realize, was usually way down near the bottom of the list.

- The personal/pedagogical intersection can be a difficult relationship to be in with your students. For instance, when I was learning to be a teacher, the very little training that we *did* get in this area consisted of a session on assertiveness training to help us in our relationships with our students and a reminder that we should walk together to the counselors with those students whose problems were beyond our abilities to help. I have made that walk a number of times. I have counseled (and referred students for more help) concerning their existential crises, drug and alcohol abuse, dysfunctional family relationships, depression, paralyzing bouts with stress, paranoia, broken hearts, and nervous breakdowns. Furthermore, the personal/pedagogical intersection can be a dangerous place to work. The one ironclad directive I was given in my first teaching position was "Never be alone with a student. Never be in a room with the door closed. Then it would be your word against his or hers. And you would lose."

- What do I remember about *my* teachers? Frankly (sadly?), I don't remember the material we studied. In fact, I don't remember most of my teachers at all. I cannot remember their names or their faces. The only ones I *can* remember are the ones I really liked and the ones I hated. I also remember the ones I fell in love with, of course, like my eighth-grade English teacher, and the ones I fantasized about, like my archaeology teacher. But the ones I really remember, the ones I have the greatest indebtedness to and respect for, are those that reached out to me, that were willing to help me with the personal crises that occasionally (but inevitably) impinged upon my schoolwork. I remember, for instance, Donald Frye, my Old English teacher, who did little more than listen to me vent my anguish over a broken relationship and my fear of my substance abuse for an hour one day, but who was also the only person I felt I could go to for help at the time. In retrospect, it is clear that my personal relationship with one concerned teacher made an invaluable difference in my life *and* kept me in school in the process.

- As English teachers, we are more likely than most teachers to become aware of our students' emotional lives and personal problems. Since most of what they study and discuss in our classes is how literary characters cope or fail to cope with *their* emotional lives and personal problems, we teachers come to be seen as interested and

knowledgeable in these areas and, moreover, as accessible, as someone our students might actually be able to talk to and want to talk to
about these areas. However, this does not mean we are prepared or
qualified to do so. In my first term of teaching, we read *Romeo and
Juliet,* which I knew and understood. What I did *not* know or understand was how to respond to my student Eileen, who came to inform
me that she was going to have to miss another couple of weeks of
class because, at age fourteen, she had to have her second abortion in
two months. Her boyfriend, she said, was twenty-three. I knew well
how to respond to literary tragedy; I didn't have a clue how to
respond to her real-life tragedy.

■ Students want to make the private, the *very* private, public. They
write things about themselves that I am *embarrassed* to read. They tell
me things about themselves that I do not want to know, that I *should
not* know. I have to warn them not to write about topics that are too
personal, too emotional, for them to handle, too private to become
public. But they do it anyway. And then I am stuck trying to figure out
how to evaluate Steve's narrative about his grandmother's death, or
Sue's story of being physically and sexually abused as a child, or
Margaret's tale of her broken heart. How can I criticize the texts of
these experiences without negating the experiences themselves, without cheapening them, without putting an insurmountable distance
between myself and the writers? The message Steve will get, no matter how I try to soften it, will be that his grandmother's death itself
rates a C; Sue will understand that her sexual abuse itself is below
average; and Margaret will construe that it is her broken heart itself
that is clichéd and needs work.

■ I have learned that when my students ask to see model papers,
when they ask me, "What is this paper supposed to look like?" what
they are really asking is, "Who am I supposed to be?" I'm supposed to
tell them who to be?! I *really* don't want such a responsibility. Or do I?
I mean, the power is seductive: the molding of young minds. I would
like to fool myself that I am only teaching them how to communicate
better in written language. But I am, in fact, telling them not just what
to think and what to do, but who to be and how to feel.

■ My writing instruction insists that students make the private and
the personal public. I sequence activities and writing assignments in
order to move my students from private to public discourse, from
writer-centered to reader-centered textuality, and to infuse the former

in the latter. I require them to announce their personal positions on controversial issues, to read their writing aloud (sometimes against their wills), to make their private selves the object of a public examination and critique. I have required them to record their private truths and thoughts they did not yet want to share in public in a journal that I nonetheless read, responded to, and even graded. I have valued and encouraged students to develop what I thought was an authentic voice, a personal voice—which, in retrospect, rewarded those students best able to spill their guts on the page for my voyeuristic enjoyment, those most willing to bare their souls, to stand emotionally naked before my gaze.

- I do share my life outside of class with my students, but I share it *outside* of class, before we officially begin our meetings. I tell them about my son, my wife, my emotional cycles, typically in response to their asking me why I haven't yet finished grading their papers. My personal life, it seems, is an intrusion into my functioning as a teacher. It is the excuse for why I am not more efficient. I tell them "I have a life outside this class, too, you know" when they sigh at me for my tardiness. Recently, I shared with them that I hadn't finished grading their papers over the weekend because, frankly, I was depressed and didn't feel like doing a damn thing. I had finally given in to three straight weeks of no sun. But I am troubled—and I am not sure why I am troubled—that I used my emotional state as an excuse for not doing my job. Somehow, obviously, I feel that my personal life and emotional state should not inhibit my functioning as a teacher. But they do. Frequently.

- When I meet someone for the first time, and we introduce ourselves, and I tell them I am an English teacher, why do I take it so personally, why does it hurt so much, when they say, as they invariably do, "You teach English? Oh, I better watch my grammar. Ha Ha! English was always my worst subject!" Why do I squirm and sigh every time my younger sister sends me a letter and not-so-jokingly apologizes for the grammar and spelling and says, "Gee, I hope you're not correcting this with a red pen. Ha Ha!" "Ha Ha!" they say, but I'm not laughing.

As I come to the end of my considerations of the personal and the emotional in teaching English, I find myself thinking of a recent survey here at Loyola University of Chicago, which revealed that students want more advising. Our students' desire for more advising was, at first, a little baffling since we teachers pride ourselves on the tremendous amounts of time we spend advising students. In taking a closer look at this desire, though, what we realized is that our students mean something quite different from what we mean by "advising." While we want to tell them what courses to take to finish their programs in a timely manner, they want advice on living. They want student-teacher interaction on a truly personal level. "What they want," one of my colleagues said, "is mothers." While some might see this want as inappropriate or wrong, it is, nonetheless, a reality. And this personal, emotional reality is the single most important thing I have learned as a teacher, the single most important thing a beginning teacher should know.

13 The Use of Journals in Teacher Development and Course Design

Brenda L. Dyer
Chuo University, Tokyo, Japan

Brenda Dyer describes the insights she gained from the students she taught one year in Tokyo, who "patiently tutored" her, through their questions, journal entries, and even cross-cultural misunderstandings, in the importance of reflection by both teachers and students and of true student-centered learning.

To view education as a social and problem-solving experience rather than the transmission of preselected and predigested knowledge represents a radical shift from the way most of us were educated. Recent educators have suggested that any syllabus, preset or not, is in the end negotiated by teachers and learners. Not what was planned, but what was learned determines a syllabus, and as Candlin (1984) points out, this can be identified only after a course is over. This may be especially intimidating for beginning teachers who bring a little theory and about sixteen years of experience as a student into their first classroom. They will inevitably be faced daily with things that fit neither the planned syllabus nor their personal schemata about what a classroom should be; multicultural classrooms will compound this sense of vertigo. An anchor in the storm is the use of journals—a teacher diary coupled with learners' response journals—which will provide rich potential for learning throughout the first year. I remember my first year of classroom teaching with mixed feelings. It was in Tokyo, at Temple University, a Philadelphia-based university with two branch campuses in Japan. More training, both professional and cross-cultural, may have eased the transition; however, tremendous learning occurred within the chaos. Four years later, I view that initial experience as one of being tutored patiently by my students.

Three experiences stand out in my mind, all of which have led me to support enthusiastically the current practices of learner-centered pedagogy and the use of teacher and learner journals. Although Japanese classrooms are notoriously teacher-centered, and students seem often passive and unquestioning, in the peculiar cross-cultural context in which we both were placed, familiar rules didn't apply, and the Japanese students were grappling as hard as their inexperienced teacher was with the limits, roles, and expectations of the foreign language/culture classroom. I taught "American Short Fiction" and "Women's Studies" in the English Language program; both of these were "bridge" courses in "English for Academic Purposes," to further develop students' English language and academic skills. For the literature course, I carefully prepared lists of questions on each story: setting, plot, conflict, character, and theme. Students read the stories at home, prepared their answers to the questions, and then discussed them in class. I noted in my own log that although the students were diligent and attentive, the classes were becoming monotonous. Did I lack the necessary charisma to make literature come alive for the students? This was the pattern for much of the semester, until one day, Naoru waited for me after class, and asked, "Where do you find those questions on the stories?" I hesitated, and then answered, "I make them up." Naoru looked at me admiringly and said, "Please teach us how to make the questions." His request startled me and was the beginning of a much more interactive, learner-centered classroom practice. It marked the phase in reflective teaching which is "the search for principles that underlie our teaching, the search for reasons which are the basis of our theory of teaching" (Bartlett 1990, 211). Why must students be given questions to "really understand" the story? To carefully lead them to my own understanding of the story? My assumption had been that they wouldn't "get" the story without that external prodding.

I asked the students to begin keeping a response journal and include questions about what they had read: These questions formed the basis of the next day's discussions. Students composed worksheets for one another on rhetorical or thematic questions. Tests were based on students' questions. Essays grew out of students' developing journal inquiries. At the end of the semester, I had to admit that for the most part, my lists of questions were not necessary for the students' understanding of the text. Carefully sequenced questioning, of course, can play an important role in any teaching; however, to encourage dependence on the external "master" or "expert's" questions is to deny students the opportunity to really interact with a text as an engaged reader. To stand in awe of both the text and the question maker is disempowering; to "learn how to make the questions" is a skill to carry into the world outside the classroom. Surely our ultimate purpose as English teachers is to become redundant—to enable students to approach text on their own and as part of an interpretative community and make meaning of it.

A more painful scenario occurred in the midst of students' "oral presentations" on poems that they had been assigned to analyze. One minute into Hiroyuki's presentation, I realized that he had misunderstood the meaning of several English words in the poem, and as a result, his interpretation was (to my mind) ludicrous! I jumped in at various points, explaining the vocabulary and redirecting his analysis. I noted in my own teaching journal that I apparently needed to check students' work and give more guidance before presentation. A few weeks passed, and then I received Hiroyuki's personal journal:

> Although I suppose I learned some things from your corrections of my oral presentation, I was very confused. Where was I during my presentation? Little by little, my classmates stopped listening to me. They looked only to the back corner, at you. If you wanted to teach that poem, why did you ask me to do it?

Hiroyuki's honest response to the experience opened up a useful dialogue between us, through his journal. It also marked what Bartlett terms a "contestation" stage in reflective teaching, which "involves a search for inconsistencies and contradictions in what we do and how we think" (1990, 212).

I reflected on my purposes in assigning the oral presentations and tried to answer Hiroyuki's question: If I had wanted to teach my meaning of the poem so badly, why did I ask him to do it? And why in front of the whole class? Should I have allowed him to complete his interpretation, based as it was on errors in the literal understanding of English vocabulary? The solution of simply "checking" students' preparation before their presentation now seemed too teacher-centered and not respectful of the learner. My approach to teaching poetry in the foreign language classroom shifted considerably after that. I chose much shorter poems and encouraged students to do intensive word-level analysis as well as more global response. Their presentations were given to their classmates in groups of four or five, with the emphasis on developing a supportive interpretative peer community of fellow readers and critics. Only after this stage would they sometimes make a formal presentation to the whole class.

My last example is the most humorous. If I had had students keep a personal/response journal in the introductory "Women's Studies" class, I may have avoided the misunderstandings which ensued as a result of cross-cultural differences. The course was a literature-based survey of images of women in literature, using the excellent collection *Images of Women in Literature,* compiled by Mary Anne Ferguson (1986). Women as "Mother," "Wife," "Sex Object," and "On a Pedestal," were the stereotypes which we identified and discussed. Unbeknownst to me, Japanese see "stereotypes" as exemplary models, and so the students misunderstood my intentions completely as I presented the various stereotypes. Imagine my shock when, in their final oral presentations, one after the other stood up and said things like, "How I long to be a woman on a pedestal," and "It is very fine to be a woman as a sex object," and "This course will help me to be a better wife and mother." They were able to identify and describe the stereotypes in the literature we read, but they weren't able to move past that to a more challenging social and personal critique. This was due to my lack of understanding of their culture and theirs of mine, and the absence of true dialogue in the classroom.

Rereading my journal, it is clear that I was uncomfortable with what I saw as a women's studies teacher's role as "feminist missionary" in a foreign land. As a result, I simply presented the material and backed off from discussion for fear of disturbing their cultural customs. Little did I know that they would then take the material and use it to support their own world view. It was far from a learner-centered classroom, with the syllabus so at odds with the learners' needs and assumptions. I was able to revise the syllabus considerably for the next semester and employed response journals as an integral part of the course. I used their response journals as a jumping off point for the following class—much in the way Paulo Freire suggests educators should intervene in the "curriculum" to allow the type of student-teacher dialogue which is a *mutual* exploration of social reality. Culture, race, gender, and class are variables in the transformative dialogue that need to be identified and reflected upon:

> In contrast with the anti-dialogical and non-communicative "deposits" of the banking method of education, the content of the problem-posing method—dialogical par excellence—is constituted and organized by the students' view of the world, where their own generative themes are found. The content thus constantly expands and renews itself. The task of the dialogical teacher in an interdisciplinary team working on the thematic universe revealed by their investigation is to re-present that universe to the people from whom he first received it—and re-present it not as a lecture but as a problem. (Freire 1993, 101).

To give "stereotyping" back to the students as a problem—what is it, why does it exist, for whose benefit, to what effect—meant bringing in cognitive psychology (e.g., schema theory), anthropology, history— and thus the course became an interdisciplinary "Images of Women in Western Culture." When I realized from student journals that in order to make sense of the "problem," they were struggling to find examples and explanations from their own Japanese culture, the course took a significant step forward and then became "Images of Women in Culture," with me providing material from the West, and the students doing research on women's issues in Japan and Asia. The result was a cross-cultural exchange and an educative interaction which was transformative for both teacher and learner. I was forced to reflect on my own assumptions about stereotyping, power relations, definitions of femininity and masculinity, the use of stereotype in art, and to see how I, too, was operating from a limited "thematic universe" of my own cultural making.

In all three of these experiences, my teaching log indicates my assumptions about the teacher's role as information holder and dispenser, despite my theoretical knowledge to the contrary from teacher training. Teacher-learner dialogue lay at the heart of the learning opportunity for me as a first-year teacher. This dialogue can, of course, be achieved orally, in class or private conferences; however, in multi- or cross-cultural settings, the response journal provides an intimate, yet nonthreatening, forum for expression. The learner journal can give the beginning teacher invaluable feedback on how the students are responding intellectually and emotionally to what is being presented in class. This helped me, in conjunction with my own teaching diary, to reflect on both the content of what I was teaching and my methodology. Teaching a new course, especially one which deals with values clarification and perspective taking, as literature and women's studies do, is an experimental undertaking; the experiment becomes riskier when it involves different cultural assumptions. To tackle this experiment as a beginning teacher requires a pioneer spirit and someone willing to give up frontier independence, lay down her guns, and dialogue with learners.

References

Bartlett, Leo. 1990. "Teacher Development through Reflective Teaching." *Second Language Teacher Education*, ed. Jack C. Richards and David Nunan. New York: Cambridge University Press.

Candlin, C. N. 1984. "Syllabus Design as a Critical Process." *ELT Documents.* No. 118. London: Pergamon Press and the British Council, Central Information Service, 29–46.

Ferguson, Mary Anne, comp. 1986. *Images of Women in Literature.* 4th ed. Boston: Houghton-Mifflin.

Freire, Paulo. 1993. *Pedagogy of the Oppressed.* New Rev. 20th Ann. Ed. Translated by Myra Bergman Ramos. New York: Continuum.

14 Becoming a Teacher of Insight: The Line with No Hook

Sean Meehan
Newark Academy, Livingston, New Jersey

Sean Meehan takes us through his own changing thinking as he attempts to become a "teacher of insight," one who teaches students how to fish rather than merely handing them fish. In the process, he learns from his own struggles as a reader and writer what his students really need in order to fish for themselves.

I no longer knew what to ask
I could tell that his line had no hook
I understood that I was to stay and eat with him

W. S. Merwin, "Finding a Teacher"

A Question

Two years ago, two weeks into my second year of teaching, I explored through an imagined dialogue in my notebook what I considered to be the foundation of my teaching:

> To the question so often asked by young students, half in frustration and half in ignorance—How is this relevant?—I answer: In teaching literature, teaching English, I am teaching a way of thinking and responding. . . . I am not (do not intend) teaching you how to read this one book, but *how* to read others like it and unlike it. I am teaching you to be a reader and writer who can make decisions that readers and writers make.

Rereading this now, I can see that I was rehearsing in my mind and notebook, like a child actively preparing to write a story, what I hoped to become as a teacher. I wanted to teach English as a fluid process, to reveal the "how" of reading and writing as a way of responding to the world. I didn't want to teach English the way it was taught to me—as a fixed body of knowledge (merely a "what") to be passed on to students. I wanted my students to leave with more than a surface view of literature. I hoped to become a teacher of insight.

As a student of literature, I had experienced insight—an intuitive vision that can delve beneath the surface—as a crucial way of understanding the work of reading and writing. As a teacher of literature, even after one year, I knew that such vision was most often neglected by the external demands of curriculum and therefore discounted by our students.

I compared Thoreau's observation in *Walden* to life in my classes: "I perceive that we inhabitants of New England live this mean life that we do because our vision does not penetrate the surface of things. We think that that *is* which *appears* to be" (1982, 177). When we present literature merely as content to be acquired, and focus attention primarily on finding and learning answers and information, we encourage our students to be satisfied with the "surface of things." Instead of learning how to question, how to participate with a work critically or sensitively, students become limited, superficial seers. "Just tell us what we need to know for the exam," I have heard my students say in the cracking voice of a mean life. I began that second year with that voice and this question in mind: How could I develop in my literature course a focus on insight? That is, how could I teach my students—as I had rehearsed it in my notebook entry—to understand the decisions readers and writers make?

My thoughts turned to Zen. I knew from my own reading of Zen Buddhism that the goal of Zen practice was the experience of insight known as *satori*. As D. T. Suzuki (1964) has written:

> The object of Zen discipline consists in acquiring a new viewpoint for looking into the essence of things. . . . This acquiring of a new viewpoint in Zen is called *satori*, deemed as intuitive looking-into, in contradistinction to intellectual and logical understanding. Whatever the definition, *satori* means the unfolding of a new world hitherto unperceived in the confusion of a dualistic mind. (88)

I began to explore the connection I perceived between the object of Zen discipline and the developing focus of my teaching. To reach *satori*, one has to move away from a focus on logical understanding toward a more intuitive way of viewing the world; practices such as sitting meditation and *koan* study serve as guides for one to make this move. I applied this to my own teaching: If I wanted my students to move toward a more intuitive way of viewing literature, I would have to provide practices, as in Zen, to guide them in this transition. Concentrating on my tenth-grade American literature course, I created a Zen-inspired practice that fall. I centered this practice around the use of a journal or writer's notebook. I established the notebook as a personal place—a type of *zendo* (place of meditation)—for students to work on questions and responses, to begin to develop their insight. I encouraged them to use their notebooks during class discussions as well as for entries that they worked on at home. One of the entries I assigned my students each week was to respond to a given *koan* and explore how it might relate to the work of literature that we were reading. The first one I borrowed from Salinger's epigraph to *Nine Stories*, the famous "What is the sound of one hand clapping?" The aim of the koan, as Suzuki explains, is to force the student to assume an inquiring attitude, one that must focus on questions rather than answers (1964, 105). This was a way, I thought, to teach my students to question and to delve beneath the surface of things.

At the same time that I was thinking of Zen and insight and the foundation of my teaching, I recalled the proverb: "Give a man a fish and you have fed him for a day; teach a man to fish and you have fed him for a lifetime." This, it seemed to me, was what my teaching of insight—the use of the notebook and the *koan* entry—was all about. Rather than feeding students the meal of a particular book, I would teach them to fish, so that they could then feed themselves. Such was my belief that fall and throughout the year.

By the end of that year, however, I perceived a frustrating problem area: There was a distinct separation between the level of insight my students developed in their notebooks, especially with the free-response entries, and the fairly undeveloped and less insightful work they accomplished with the formal writing that I had assigned, their responses on essays and tests. I had taught the students to fish, perhaps, but they were fishing on a separate bank from where I stood and wanted them to stand. The question I took with me into the summer concerned this apparent gap: How could I bridge the difference?

A Response

I uncovered a response for my question that summer as I worked on my own reading and writing while participating in the Writing Institute at Teachers College. I write "uncovered" because, as I learned, I held the answer (and the problem) within my own teaching practice. One of my lessons came from reading Nancie Atwell's *In The Middle* (1987), the story of the changes she made in her approach to teaching writing and reading. She writes, in a passage concerning her own teaching foundation,

> Our kids are learning from us. The question is, what exactly are they learning? What inadvertent messages do we transmit via the standard approach to literature? I've started to try to make explicit the tacit lessons I learned as a student of literature—and to uncover the demonstrations my own teaching probably put across to those other students of literature for too many years. (152)

Reading Atwell's story, I realized that my students had learned from me, indeed; the problem concerned what I was and was not teaching. While encouraging and expecting my students to develop insight as writers and readers, I failed to provide the structure and environment (outside of the notebook writing) that writers and readers need. At best, in mixing the more radical intentions of the notebook with a traditional approach to literature (the assigned essays, most especially), I provided an environment of ambiguous footing. The rift I had perceived was implicit in my teaching. As I participated in a writing workshop at the institute, I began to explore how a workshop approach could strengthen the ground of my own classes. Atwell argues that there are three necessities for any writer, and thus three essential requirements for a writing workshop: ownership, response, and time (1987, 54). I transformed the environment of my tenth-grade course this past fall—one year after the notebook rehearsal with which I began this story—focusing on these three areas.

Ownership

In the first several weeks of the fall term, I established the centrality of the notebooks in the course. The crucial difference from the previous year was that the centrality, this time, radiated from the student. I did not assign topics or questions for notebook entries, nor the type of writing that students should do in those entries. Instead, I assigned writing; I required students to be responsible for at least three entries per week completed outside of class, in addition to the entries (about three per week) worked on during writing workshop. Giving students responsibility for their responses was not an easy task at first, but for developing writers it was an educational necessity. As a developing writer myself, I know this much: Meaningful writing (and meaningful learning of writing) grows from a personal engagement with the topic. Participating in the workshop last summer, I realized that to write well, perhaps at all, I must have a stake in what I write. I translated this understanding of ownership into my teaching. As a result, the notebook became a more authentic, personal space for students to explore and develop their own insights and interests (and not mine) as writers and readers.

I extended this foundation of ownership to include the pieces that students developed from their entries. I removed the assigned five-page essays (with which all of us are familiar) and in their place, once again, I assigned writing. Three weeks into the term the first project was due: a finished piece of writing, topic and genre and length to be decided by the student. I think this worked especially well as an introduction to the writing workshop; it gave students the room to stretch their writing muscles and explore their reach. For the second project of the term I assigned the genre, the traditional literary critical essay; students, however, were responsible for the topic and the focus of this essay. While studying this genre as *one* type of response to literature, we explored various examples of critical essays—something I had not done previously when I repeatedly assigned this type of essay.

The year before I was frustrated with the lack of insight and personal connections in my students' essay writing. Those essays were well structured but, from my point of view, bare and undeveloped. Having seen the type of writing that students will accomplish when allowed to make writing decisions, it is clear to me now that I obstructed my students that year from connecting their notebook with their finished writing pieces. I created the separation by giving the same type of essay assignments that I was given, the type I assumed one needed in order to learn about writing. My assignments worked like a broken bridge. I hear the question I once raised myself: How can we let students write whatever they want—how on earth will this lead to good writing? We can let students make such decisions, as I have learned, if we want them to develop as writers. I think of X. J. Kennedy's comment: "Good writing occurs because a writer passionately desires to say something. Students do not need more abstract advice about how to write. They need somehow to have their feelings kindled" (Atwell 1987, 148). Students need guidance and support to develop their writing, yes—but the type of support that is not the spoon-feeding of assignments. My students needed the strong kindling of being asked to say what they have to say.

Response

Students learning to write with insight and skill also need response to develop what it is they have to say. This is true of any writer, myself included. During the final days of the Writing Institute workshop last summer, I struggled with the piece that was due at the final class, a short memoir whose direction was unclear to me. I learned during a peer-response group that my work had two different strands within it; hearing this response, I was able to see the difference and decide finally on the direction in which I wanted the writing to go. In my classes this fall, I established response during the writing process as a foundation in the course. During the writing time of every writing workshop, I spent my time conferring with students, providing them with an avenue of response. A second avenue was the peer-response groups which met at the end of workshop approximately twice each week. In both cases, students received verbal response and guidance for their writing during the process itself. This is the point at which I was able to "kindle" the instincts and interests of my students, as well as learn what aspects of writing we needed to work on further. I stopped writing marginal comments on finished pieces; by that point, because of the verbal responses they had received, my students knew where they needed to go with their writing.

Two years ago I sensed the value of the writing conference for the developing writer; I wanted to incorporate this into my approach to teaching writing. I didn't succeed, however, because though I wanted to teach the process of writing, I emphasized (and mainly taught) only its product. I created yet another gap by grading only the finished product of my students' writing, which was, in many cases, a first draft. Looking back on that year, I can agree with Donald Murray's assertion: "Classes in which we give assignments and grade first drafts produce the kind of writing we deplore." (1982, 150) This past term, instead of deplorable writing, I found my students writing more thoroughly, with greater commitment to developing their work. I encouraged this commitment by evaluating the entire process that leads to a piece of finished writing. I gave the notebook a grade for the term, having checked it approximately every two weeks. I evaluated the effort and commitment that students put into their notebook work, not the content of their entries. In the case of a writing project, I evaluated the finished piece in relation to the work—the ideas and drafts and revision—that had created it. I kept a record of the progress of each student with a given project. By the time I read a finished piece,

I knew where the writing stood because I was aware (and involved) with the work that stood behind it. And so were my students: Along with each finished piece, I required my students to turn in a brief process log in which they recounted (and relived) the story of the work of their writing. My evaluation of the process of writing, rather than the product, reinforced for students the reality that writing is a creative process, that final drafts do not happen miraculously but are developed through work. The previous year I taught my students to be frustrated with their writing because I implied that writers do create miraculously, after one draft, like a Moses standing in awe before the burning bush.

Time

Rather than Moses, I believe in Jacob as an authentic model for the developing writer.

> Jacob was left alone, and a man wrestled with him there till daybreak. When the man saw that he could not get the better of Jacob, he struck him in the hollow of his thigh, so that Jacob's hip was dislocated as they wrestled. The man said, "Let me go, for day is breaking," but Jacob replied, "I will not let you go unless you bless me." The man asked, "What is your name?" "Jacob," he answered. The man said, "Your name shall no longer be Jacob but Israel, because you have striven with God and with mortals, and have prevailed. (Genesis 32:24–28)

Jacob's lesson for us is that writers struggle through their search for meaning. Young writers, learning to wrestle, need the time and space of Jacob if they are going to prevail. With Jacob in mind, I cleared plenty of space in the course for my students to engage in this creative struggle. The heart of the writing workshop was a fifteen- to twenty-minute writing period: This is the time when students worked on their writing—notebook entries, drafts, conferences. Most important about this time was its predictability; the workshop became a set place where students expected to work on their writing. Prior to this fall term, I had expected students to work on their writing at home—why waste class time with work they can do elsewhere, I had been taught to believe. The problem is that developing writers don't learn "elsewhere"; they learn within a context that reinforces their writing. There should be no better learning context than the classroom. As a basketball coach, I would never expect my players to learn the sport primarily outside of the time we have to practice. Donald Murray's statement makes great sense to this basketball player: "It is our job as teachers of writing to create a context that is as appropriate for writing as the gym is for basketball" (Atwell 1987, 54).

I further developed this context for writing by giving students the time that is needed for a writer to make the journey from an idea to its final destination. For both writing projects this past fall, I set a publication deadline, a date when finished pieces were presented to the class; I also gave guidelines during the process, when students should begin to draft, to revise, to edit. Within this structure, I allowed my students the time—it varied with the student and the project; that's the point—that is needed to do what Natalie Goldberg calls, in a rich metaphor, "composting": "It takes time. Continue to turn over and over the organic details of your life until some of them fall through the garbage of discursive thoughts to the solid ground of black soil" (1986, 14). To write this article I needed time: to turn over ideas, to draft, to revise, to throw away, to draft again. This is what I know as a writer, what I read in the determined patience of Jacob. How could I, as a teacher, expect my students to write with less time than I would accept for myself? I am astounded to realize that this is what I asked my students to do—until this year—when I only set due dates without clearing space and time for writing. How?

I know one reason why this could happen: the tightening feeling of anxiety. For the writer, time is a necessity; for the teacher, time is most often a constraint. In my case, the constraint involved my primary responsibility to teach literature and not just writing. With only one class per day for both reading and writing, I felt justified in raising this question: How can I let my students have more time to write when I have all these books to cover? Last summer I was excited by the thought of developing a writing workshop, but thoroughly anxious with my concern to incorporate this with a "literature-based" course. I was staring, it seemed, into another rift. Once again, I uncovered both the problem and the solution from within my own teaching. Nancie Atwell reminded me:

> When we look at our processes as readers and reflect on appropriate methods for teaching reading, it's hard to justify truncating reading into a lecture-assign-evaluate lockstep, just as reflections on our writing dismantled a similar monolith. For in truth, both writing and reading are written language *processes.* (1987, 155)

When I reflected on my own work as a reader, I realized that I had not been teaching reading as I had wanted to, as a process—encouraging my students to "make the decisions readers make." In truth, I neither needed nor wanted to "cover" books, yet this is what I was doing. This past fall I stopped "covering" books—stopped feeding my students for the day and truly began to teach them reading. I followed Atwell's lead and created a reading environment that complemented the written-language process of the writing workshop.

I cleared away the time-consuming, lockstep approach to books that I had perfected in my first two years. In its place I established a more fluid, workshop approach to reading literature, one that focused on two crucial changes. The first change concerned the assignment of reading: When reading a given work of literature, I assigned a due date for when that reading should be completed. I devoted one class each week to a reading workshop, a time when we interwove our writing more consciously with what we had been reading: Here, students worked in their notebooks and in peer-response groups to develop their understanding and insight concerning the work of literature; here, I focused my attention on teaching strategies for reading, interpreting, and responding to such a work of literature—not just covering and getting through that particular book. This past fall, for the first time, I charged my students with the responsibility to read. A second change in my approach reinforced this responsibility. As much as I could, I connected the genre of the writing we worked on with the genre of the literature we were reading. For example, when we studied the literary critical essay, we read as many examples of the genre as I could find. In the winter and spring we will study—read and write—memoir and poetry; I hope to give students greater responsibility in choosing their own texts within the given genre. Like a writer and a reader turning over meaning, I am still working on cultivating this important connection. From my vantage point of one term, the positive result of this approach was that I encouraged students to participate more fully within the literature that they read. In this way the processes of reading and writing—what I wanted to teach them—became more accessible, the learning more possible.

An Understanding

Two years ago, two weeks into my second year of teaching, I began my refusal to approach English as though I were feeding my students for the day. Instead, I would teach them to read and write with the insight to feed themselves for a lifetime. This was my teaching foundation, as I perceived it, and it still is. But what I have learned about that foundation is that two years ago I had not explored the ground beneath my teaching feet so thoroughly, had not turned over the earth on which I was standing. Last summer I engaged in the crucial work of composting. While participating in the workshop, as I have mentioned, I also stumbled upon a W. S. Merwin poem, "Finding a Teacher," that I had read the previous year, but in a different light. The poem ends with these lines:

> I no longer knew what to ask
> I could tell that his line had no hook
> I understood that I was to stay and eat with him

In rereading this poem, having explored my own assumptions about teaching—with thoughts of fishing—I focused anew on the strange and simple ending. The lack of a hook, I understood, is an important aspect of the teaching that takes place within the poem. It is crucial because in its absence, the work of the teacher, the fishing in which he or she has achieved a special skill, does not overwhelm the student. Rather, the line with no hook teaches the student to respect the process of the fishing; it is through this respect that the student can know and tell and understand for him- or herself. When I leave the poem, I imagine the two, student and teacher, sharing together a meal of fresh insight.

I look back now on my first attempt to teach insight with an understanding of where I lost my way. I don't consider the Zen inspiration to have been a gimmick. My intention was strong and well informed—students do need practice to develop insight. Unfortunately, I did not, as a teacher, put into practice my own beliefs. Because of my lingering, standard approach to literature, my students that year did not engage truly in the practice of writing and reading: At best, my students struggled with my questions and insights, not their own. Practice requires time, response, and ownership to be carried out thoroughly. It is only this past fall that I have begun to establish an environment in which such practice can take place. I have reached this insight concerning my own teaching: It is not enough to teach students to fish, because there remains the possibility that we as teachers will only teach them the way we have learned to fish. We may not feed our students for the day, but we end up, in effect, fishing in their place. In this case, some skills or knowledge may be passed on, but our students will not reach an understanding of things, the depth of the reading and writing through which they have been coursing.

With the workshop approach that I have initiated, I am teaching my students to fish, using a line with no hook. I will not give them the insight that I have—I know that last summer I could not be given this understanding of my own teaching; it came through work and practice with my own reading and writing. This is the way I continue to become a teacher of insight. Teaching by a deep stream, I encourage my students to sit down and learn with me.

References

Atwell, Nancie. 1987. *In the Middle: Writing, Reading, and Learning with Adolescents.* Upper Montclair, NJ: Boynton/Cook.

Goldberg, Natalie. 1986. *Writing Down the Bones: Freeing the Writer Within.* Boston: Shambhala.

Merwin, W. S. 1988. *Selected Poems.* New York: Atheneum.

Murray, Donald. 1982. *Learning by Teaching: Selected Articles on Writing and Teaching.* Upper Montclair, NJ: Boynton/Cook.

Probst, Robert E. 1992. Writing from, of, and about Literature. *Reader Response in the Classroom: Evoking and Interpreting Meaning in Literature,* ed. Nicholas J. Karolides. New York: Longman.

Salinger, J. D. 1953. *Nine Stories.* Boston: Little, Brown.

Suzuki, D. T. 1964. *An Introduction to Zen Buddhism.* New York: Grove Press.

Thoreau, Henry David. 1982. *Walden and Other Writings.* Edited by Joseph Wood Krutch. New York: Bantam.

15 "Are You Listening to Me?" Effective Evaluation of Student Writing

Janet Gebhart Auten
American University

Janet Gebhart Auten looks at ways of bridging the gap between how teachers evaluate their students' writing and the ways in which students understand those evaluations, offering the results of two questionnaires designed to explore the experiences and expectations of both groups.

I feel as if I have been searching for years for the right questions, questions which would establish a tone of master and apprentice, no, the voice of a fellow craftsman having a conversation about a piece of work, writer to writer, neither praise nor criticism but questions which imply further drafts, questions which draw helpful comments out of the student writer.

Donald Murray

Evaluating student writing may seem to a beginning teacher to be like voodoo: it affects students in mysterious and unpredictable ways—and nobody can define exactly how it is done. The literature on evaluating and commenting on student writing offers useful analysis and supportive advice,[1] but no "surefire" recipe for an effective way to make evaluation meaningful to students. Beginning teachers may see themselves addressing a stack of student essays as if talking into a void, carrying out a meaningless but necessary task of marking in the margins. Connors and Lunsford's (1993) recent survey of teachers commenting on student papers suggests "not so much that teachers had nothing to say as that they had little time or energy to say it and little faith that what they had to say would be heard" (211). Finding an evaluative voice that will be "heard" seems to be a matter of long experience, or timing, or some special trick. It would take a witchdoctor to find the formula.

All of us who teach may wish for some witchcraft at times, yet evaluation can be a meaningful rather than mysterious way to interact with students. By understanding and acknowledging their role as evaluators and the rhetorical nature of their comments on student writing, teachers can demystify evaluation and clarify communication both for themselves and for their students.

Working with graduate student teachers of college writing has shown me that beginning teachers at any level need confidence in evaluation as much as strategies and style. They can cultivate assurance that students will "hear" their message by developing two kinds of awareness: an awareness of the context in which they evaluate and comment on papers, and an understanding of the attitudes and assumptions of their student "audience."

The Teacher as Evaluator: The Context of Commenting

Beginning teachers need to be aware of the context of expectations and intentions in which they evaluate students' papers. For one thing. evaluation is not just "grading" but a response to students, an integral part of their task as teachers. As literary theorist Barbara Herrnstein Smith (1983) affirms, evaluations "are among the most fundamental forms of social communication" (20). Whether they are commenting on intermediate drafts or grading final drafts, teachers invariably express an *evaluation* whenever they respond to student writing. What's more, this evaluative ingredient affects the nature of their communication with students.

Teachers' preconceptions exert a powerful influence over their experience of a student text. As Smith (1987) points out, labels such as "literature" or "art" affect any reader, "shaping our experience of . . . value" (451). The label "student writing" shapes the teacher's expectations of its possibilities and functions as a work of an apprentice writer. Whereas most readers assume that the text they read is deliberately crafted as a "finished" work of an author, teachers of writing typically assume the student text is imperfect, unfinished, fashioned by a novice. They come to reading with the purpose of *assisting* the writer. Whereas "normal" readers will work to overcome interference with their comprehension, in reading to evaluate student writing, teachers focus on that interference (*cf.,* Williams; Harris; Searle and Dillon). Moreover, in evaluating school-sponsored (assigned) writing, teachers are not just "collaborative readers" who give helpful feedback, but "surrogates for the academic prose reader" (McCracken 1985, 275). As Freedman (1979; 1987) found, evaluators tend to try to match students' writing to their perceptions of how academic discourse should "sound." Evaluation tells students how well they have communicated. But the teacher's comments, which support and/or justify that evaluation, tend to express how well the student's writing matched the teacher's expectations.

"Why can they speak and get their views across so well but not write and get them across?" a graduate student teacher asked me. Lara (not her real name) was sitting in my office after her second "teaching day" with my class of first-year college writers. On my desk was the stack of student essays which she had been reading over the weekend. "I had very high expectations going in" to the paper pile, she confessed. On the basis of class discussions she had observed in my classroom and later led herself, this beginning teacher had formed an idea of the kind of papers she would find when she sat down to read these essays. She described how she had created a "perfect" environment for the project: a clean desk, neatly organized piles of papers, assignments, grading sheets, and well-sharpened pencils. "I was ready to *grade,*" she chuckled ruefully. But as she read, Lara became more and more disturbed. Struck by the difference in students' class performance and their writing, she "had to adjust" her expectations.

But the adjustment undercut Lara's confidence in her ability to evaluate the students "fairly." Because she had to alter her expectations for essays and her assumptions about the students, she worried that she had graded them "too harshly." Like most beginning English teachers, Lara is an able writer who is unsure not only of the abilities of student writers, but of her own ability to evaluate their writing. After we compared notes, Lara saw that her evaluations were similar to mine and closely matched the grades and comments the students eventually received on their papers. But Lara's problem lay in her lack of a clear sense of her expectations as an evaluator. She discovered that although she had assumed she "would be a pushover grader, it was just the opposite. Because my expectations were high, I was tougher than I thought."

Lara's reactions illustrate a fact that we often overlook—or try to ignore—that evaluation necessarily incorporates the subjectivity of the evaluator. As Lara commented, "You can only be completely objective if you don't care—and this is a caring profession." However, as Lara also found, effective evaluation depends on more than a well-organized desk top. Evaluators need to define their expectations clearly, both for themselves and their students. Written evaluation/expectation guidelines can provide a framework for teachers' judgments and students' revisions. Such a guide sheet might offer the teacher's expectations for an assignment and indicate what he or she will "look for" (the basis of judgment) in evaluating the students' writing.

Students as Audience: The Context of Reading

Yet evaluation challenges teachers to be aware not only of their context for evaluating, but also of the different context in which the student reads that evaluation. In writing comments on students' papers, for example, a teacher may intend to appear as a coach or even, as Donald Murray puts it, a "fellow craftsman." However, the teacher may appear to a student simply as a judge. Studies suggest that while teachers may see comments as a way to help students revise and improve their writing, students may read comments as guides for "what to fix" (Danis 1987; Freedman 1987)[2] or as an authoritative intrusion, a text which suggests that the writer's message needs "help." For teachers, the context of commenting involves intentions to affect student behavior, to move their audience positively to revise and improve their writing.[3] However, students' context for reading may center on the teacher's presence as paper grader and involve negative views of teacher comments as criticism rather than encouragement. A student's attitude about writing and about teacher evaluation affects the delicate balance between what the teacher will need to make explicit and what need not be explained when the teacher writes comments on the student's paper.

My own surveys of first-year college writing students about their attitudes toward English/writing classes and the comments they have received on their writing show that students come into a writing class with firm expectations and attitudes about teacher evaluation. While students generally have a positive outlook about writing and express both interest and desire for teachers' comments, many of the students in my surveys remember specific comments which "seemed sarcastic," and teachers' questions which, as one student put it, made them "become so personally insulted that [they could] see no way of improving." Several of the students in my surveys have mentioned the common "Can you write a clearer sentence?" type of question as one that sounds ridiculous in their context of reading, and they retort, "If I knew the right way, I wouldn't have gotten it wrong in the first place."

But teachers' reactions to these student responses are equally illuminating. One instructor said, "I guess I always took it for granted that students were interpreting my comments in the way I intended." Many are surprised that students apparently assume teachers will be more judgmental and less encouraging than the teacher intends to be. Students' preoccupation with such judgments results from their past experiences with teacher responses to their writing. As Nancy Sommers (1982) points out, if students have found most teacher comments reflect concern for correctness, concern for correctness will dominate their interpretations of teacher evaluation of their writing. Without some means of ascertaining student attitudes, teachers are left to guess what students' experiences and assumptions about evaluation are.

Moreover, most students are not only inexperienced writers, but inexperienced readers who may not have the strategies to interpret evaluative comments (*cf.,* Ziv; Gee; and Auten). Studies by King (1979) and Smith (1987) indicate that many students—at all levels—simply do not know how to interpret teachers' comments on their writing and don't know how to use comments to improve. They may simply take negative comments as personal criticism (Gee 1972). Moreover, a student reader sees the teacher's evaluation as a whole—and has few or no textual cues concerning which comments are more important than others. Therefore student readers may need to be given some instruction about the teacher's intentions in evaluating and writing comments—from reacting as "audience" to judging effectiveness. In class discussions, students and teachers should explore their respective expectations and assumptions about evaluation. In addition, the evaluator could suggest appropriate responses to comments, the strategies for dealing with the kinds of comments students encounter most often. Teachers need to share enough of their "teacherly" concerns to empower students—not only to deal with evaluations effectively, but also to become able evaluators of their own writing.

Great Expectations: Recognizing and Reconciling Contexts

Beginning teachers have an advantage as evaluators because they have recently been students themselves. Whether undergraduate or graduate students, younger or older, beginning teachers have fresh in their minds the effect of teachers' comments and corrections on their own papers. This recollection can be captured on paper and used as a guide to the teacher's context for evaluating student writing, just as a student survey can be used to assess the audience for evaluation.

The attitude survey I had used for students (see Appendix A) proved to be a useful tool with which to compare the views of beginning teachers and a group of the students they would be teaching. I administered the questionnaire to two classes of graduate students preparing to teach English in secondary schools and colleges, asking them to respond not as teachers but as students remembering comments they have received on their writing. At the same time, I surveyed two first-semester college writing classes, the students who would later meet these student teachers in the classroom. The results (see Appendix B) revealed interesting disparities in outlook as well as some revealing points of agreement between prospective teachers and their students.

Among the twenty-four graduate students preparing to teach, I found more uniform responses and, not surprisingly, more confidence in writing and revising than among the thirty-eight undergraduate respondents. However, the undergraduates apparently had more confidence in the effectiveness of teacher comments than the teachers did. Almost two-thirds of the students (63 percent) and less than one-half of the teachers (42 percent) thought that teachers' comments were always or often helpful in improving their writing.

Two other revealing comparisons suggest a gap in expectations between teachers and students. Whereas the beginning teachers overwhelmingly focused on the importance of an inclusive note at the end of a paper, students were just as apt to look for marginal comments and personal remarks addressed to them. The opinions of teachers and students about "the best reason for comments" varied even more significantly. While almost half of the beginning teachers chose "clarifying a point" as the best purpose for commenting, student choices varied widely, with the largest percentage choosing "to point out changes" as the evaluator's most important purpose.

The narrative comments given at the end of the questionnaire, however, showed that teachers and students may have a good foundation of shared experiences and common views of evaluation. Asked to recall their experiences with teachers' evaluations, graduate student teachers echoed comments made by students in my surveys. One beginning teacher remarked, "My most memorable comments are the ones that were most cutting: 'What in the world do you mean?' and 'Why do you think this is relevant?'" Another commented, "I most dislike teachers who give a grade which is supported by neither marks on the paper nor a written comment at the end." And a third thought, "Personal agreement or disagreement comments lend a personal touch, which shows the teacher read and thought about" the paper.

The narrative comments from the student surveys were remarkably similar. One student remembered getting a paper back "and all I could see were the red marks. I was completely frustrated and I had no confidence in my writing, and it still haunts me when writing a paper." Another commented that "If I got a paper back with no comments, I would feel that the teacher skimmed the paper and just placed a grade on it with little care or effort." And a third student expressed a desire for personal comments from the teacher, concluding that "I like it when a teacher writes down if you did something they liked, instead of just marking the wrong things." As this representative sample shows, both teachers and students recognize the value of positive, personal evaluative comments.

These disparities and similarities in perceptions and expectations provide a useful basis for clarifying communication about evaluation. After assessing their own assumptions as well as those of their students, teachers can work to remedy differences, bringing evaluation into class discussion and offering students a glimpse of their teacher's personal experiences and expectations in evaluating writing. The natural verbal abilities of most English teachers set them apart from many of their students. As one student teacher wrote on the survey form: "Most of the comments that I have received from teachers have been good . . . Most teachers like my writing." Moreover, beginning teachers' training in recent composition theory tells them that writing is always "in process," while students still often view their papers as final products, "written in stone," and teachers as judges whose evaluation is embodied in a grade rather than communicated in comments. Therefore, the challenge for teachers in evaluating students' writing is not just to be "clear" or "audience aware," but to reconcile their context for writing comments with students' awareness and ability to interpret teachers' evaluations. Teachers need to communicate their expectations before they read papers and then offer reasons for their comments and their strategies for using them. That type of communication will establish a common context of assumptions and associations in which both teachers and their student audience can make evaluation meaningful.

Notes

1. Some representative studies are Brannon and Knoblauch's "On Students' Rights to Their Own Texts: A Model of Teacher Response"; Jean Anne King, "Teachers' Comments on Students' Writing: A Conceptual

Analysis and Empirical Study"; Nancy McCracken's dissertation "Teachers' Response to Students' Writing: A Description of the Process as Teaching, Problem-Solving, Reading, and Composing"; and Nancy Sommers's "Responding to Student Writing." Sommers's studies of actual teacher comments (1982) indicate that comments can send mixed messages with confused purposes, which make revision a "guessing game," as she puts it, for students. Zirinsky (1977) and Butler (1980) point out that, often, teachers' assumptions and motives for commenting are incomprehensible to students.

2. Danis (1987) casts herself in the role of a "collaborator—a midwife, a coach" rather than a judge. Yet her research shows that her commenting persona was at odds with her students' expectations: Students don't expect "conversations about their writing," she notes. "They simply assume . . . that we're going to show them what's wrong" (19). Freedman (1987) blames this attitude on conditioning: After years of schooling, students are "product-oriented and grade-oriented . . . writing mostly in order to play the school game" (38).

3. Sommers's (1982) study discusses three ways in which teachers can prompt students to revise: (1) by dramatizing the presence of a reader; (2) by helping students become readers of their own writing; and (3) by showing students if their writing communicates effectively. Lutz (1980) points out that comments vary according to the commentor's attitude toward the student's text, as appraising, prescribing, or challenging. Purves (1984) makes a similar classification, with four categories: responding, judging, analyzing, and improving. Greenhalgh (1992) recasts response in terms of "voice" rather than role, differentiating between appeals to "external authority" and reflections of the teacher's "reading experience" (405).

References

Auten, Janet G. 1992. "How Students Read Us: Audience Awareness and Teacher Commentary on Writing." *The Writing Instructor* 11 (Winter): 83–94.

Brannon, Lil, and C. H. Knoblauch. 1992. "On Students' Rights to their Own Texts: A Model of Teacher Response." *College Composition and Communication* 33 (May): 157–66.

Butler, John F. 1980. "Remedial Writers: The Teacher's Job as Corrector of Papers." *College Composition and Communication* 31: 270–77.

Connors, Robert J., and Andrea A. Lunsford. 1993. "Teachers' Rhetorical Comments on Student Papers." *College Composition and Communication* 44 (May): 200–23.

Danis, M. Francine. 1987. "The Voice in the Margins: Paper-Marking as Conversation." *Freshman English News* 15: 18–20.

Freedman, Sarah Warshauer. 1979. "How Characteristics of Student Essays Influence Teachers' Evaluations." *Journal of Educational Psychology* 71 (3): 328–38.

———. 1987. "Recent Developments in Writing: HowTeachers Manage Response." *English Journal* 76: 35–40.

Gee, Thomas C. 1972. "Students' Responses to Teacher Comments." *Research in the Teaching of English* 6: 212–19.

Greenhalgh, Anne M. 1992. "Voices in Response: A Postmodern Reading of Teacher Response." *College Composition and Communication* 43 (October): 401–10.

Harris, Winifred Hall. 1977. "Teacher Response to Student Writing: A Study of the Response Patterns of High School English Teachers to Determine the Basis for Teacher Judgment of Student Writing." *Research in the Teaching of English* 11 (Fall): 175–85.

King, Jean Anne. 1980. Teachers' Comments on Students' Writing: A Conceptual Analysis and Empirical Study. Ph.D. diss., Cornell University, 1979. Abstract in *Dissertation Abstracts International* 40: 4872A.

Lutz, Evelyn Marie. 1980. Classification of Teacher Written Communications on Student Assignments. Ph.D. diss., Case Western Reserve University, 1980. Abstract in *Dissertation Abstracts International* 41: 1375.

McCracken, Nancy Mellin. 1985. Teachers' Response to Students' Writing: A Description of the Process as Teaching, Problem-Solving, Reading, and Composing. Ph.D. Diss., New York University.

Murray, Donald M. 1979. "The Listening Eye: Reflections on the Writing Conference." *College English* 41: 13–18. Rpt. in *Rhetoric and Composition: A Sourcebook for Teachers and Writers*, ed. Richard L. Graves. Upper Montclair, NJ: Boynton/Cook, 1984. 263–68.

Purves, Alan. 1984. "The Teacher as Reader: An Anatomy." *College English* 46: 259–65.

Searle, Dennis, and David Dillon. 1980. "The Message of Marking: Teacher Written Responses to Student Writing at Intermediate Grade Levels." *Research in the Teaching of English* 16: 233–42.

Smith, Barbara Herrnstein. 1983. "Contingencies of Value." *Critical Inquiry* 10 (Sep.): 1–32.

———. 1987. "Value/Evaluation." *South Atlantic Quarterly* 86: 445–56.

Sommers, Nancy. 1982. "Responding to Student Writing." *College Composition and Communication* 33: 148–56.

Williams, Joseph. 1981. "The Phenomenology of Error." *College Composition and Communication* 32: 152–68.

Zirinsky, Hendriekje B. 1977. An Investigation of Student Awareness of Teacher Criteria for Evaluating Writing as an Element in the Composing Process. Ph.D. diss., University of North Carolina, 1977. Abstract in *Dissertation Abstracts International* 37: 168A.

Ziv, Nina. 1984. "The Effect of Teacher Comments on the Writing of Four College Freshmen." *New Directions in Composition Research*, eds. Richard Beach and Lillian Bridwell. New York: Guilford.

APPENDIX A

Student Survey Form

Your Name _____

This is a survey of your attitudes toward writing in general and "school" writing in particular. It is not a "test": There are no "right" answers. You will not be penalized for honesty, nor will you get a better grade in this course if you say "nice" things about teachers. The responses you give will simply help me get to know "where you are" and as a result—I hope— better help you with your writing.

Also, this survey is part of a larger, ongoing research project for which results are used anonymously (names removed) as "data" to help other teachers know students' attitudes better. Your time and cooperation are greatly appreciated.

I. Think of your recent experiences with classes in which "writing" was taught, and circle the letter of the one best answer for each of the following questions:

1. How would you rate your past experiences in English classes in terms of their effect on your writing?
    a. very positive
    b. positive
    c. adequate
    d. negative
    e. very negative

2. How often are teachers' comments on your papers really helpful to your writing?
    a. always
    b. often
    c. sometimes
    d. rarely
    e. never

3. As a writer of essays and papers for classes, how would you rate yourself?
    a. excellent
    b. good
    c. average
    d. fair
    e. poor

4. How would you rate your attitude toward writing in general?
    a. Very positive, confident
    b. Positive
    c. Neutral, don't know
    d. Somewhat negative
    e. Very negative, not confident

5. How would you rate your ability to revise your writing?
   a. Good
   b. Fair
   c. Poor
   d. Terrible

II. Now turn your attention to the issue of comments on student writing. Please take a few minutes to answer the following questions, choosing *one* best answer to each question. Then simply sign the statement at the bottom. Thank you for your time and effort.

1. When I hand in an assigned paper. I hope the teacher will
   a. read it several times and make comments on both content and correctness.
   b. read it several times and mark everything that needs fixing.
   c. read it carefully but not critically.
   d. read it quickly to get my point and give me a grade.
   e. read it over for content but ignore things like spelling errors and typos.

2. I think that a teacher can be most helpful to me by
   a. marking every mistake on the paper.
   b. marking only a few of the major problems in the paper.
   c. not marking the paper—giving me comments orally.
   d. not marking on the paper—just giving one long comment at the end.

3. When I get back a paper, the first thing I look for (after I look at the grade) is
   a. a note at the end.
   b. comments in the margins.
   c. a stated explanation for the grade.
   d. personal notes addressed to me.
   e. how much the teacher has written on the paper.

4. From my experience with assigned papers, I think the best reason for comments on papers is [remember, pick only one!]
   a. to show the reason for the grade.
   b. to show the mistakes you made.
   c. to help you clarify a point you are trying to make.
   d. To point out places that need changing.
   e. To show you what is good about your writing.
   f. To show where the reader gets confused.
   g. To show you what is bad about your writing.

Now—last but not least, what are *your comments* about teachers' comments? What are the most memorable comments you have received [good or bad]? What kinds of comments do you most appreciate? (Please write below or on the back of this sheet.)

APPENDIX B

*Survey of Attitudes on Commenting**

1992, 1993 First-semester writing classes—38 students.
Summer 1993 and Fall 1993 Graduate student classes—24 students.

	CW students	GRAD students
1. Experiences in English classes—effect on your writing?		
a. very positive	5 (13%)	8 (33%)
b. positive	16 (42%)	11 (46%)
c. adequate	12 (32%)	5 (21%)
d. negative	5 (13%)	0
e. very negative	0	0
2. Comments on papers really helpful to your writing?		
a. always	11 (29%)	4 (17%)
b. often	13 (34%)	6 (25%)
c. sometimes	12 (32%)	12 (50%)
d. rarely	2 (5%)	2 (8%)
e. never	0	0
3. How would you rate yourself as writer?		
a. excellent	2 (5%)	6 (25%)
b. good	15 (39%)	17 (71%)
c. average	18 (47%)	1 (4%)
d. fair	3 (8%)	0
4. Ability to revise your writing?		
a. good	6 (16%)	16 (67%)
b. fair	24 (63%)	7 (29%)
c. poor	6 (16%)	1 (4%)
d. terrible	2 (5%)	0
5. The first thing I look for is		
a. a note at the end.	14 (37%)	16 (67%)
b. the comments in the margins.	11 (29%)	5 (21%)
c. a stated reason for the grade.	2 (5%)	0
d. personal notes.	6 (16%)	2 (8%)
e. how much teacher has written.	3 (8%)	1 (4%)
6. The best reason for comments on papers is		
a. to show the reason for the grade.	6 (16%)	3 (13%)
b. to show the mistakes you made.	6 (16%)	0
c. to help clarify a point.	8 (21%)	11 (46%)
d. to point out changes to be made.	12 (32%)	2 (8%)
e. to show what is good.	1 (3%)	6 (25%)
f. to show how to fix mistakes.	1 (3%)	1 (4%)
g. to show what is bad.	2 (5%)	1 (4%)

* Excerpted from the survey which used the form shown in Appendix A.

16 Out of Ashes

Inga Harmon Smith
Communications Unlimited, Columbus, Ohio

Inga Harmon Smith outlines Project BOOST, a system of incentives and rewards she developed to motivate the seemingly apathetic vocational students she found herself working with when she returned to teaching after a twenty-year hiatus—students who responded in ways she would never have imagined.

Back in the "Dark Ages" (the early 1950s), when I first started teaching, things were different from what they are now. Students usually did what they were asked to do, and if they didn't like it, few were inclined to create a scene by refusing. Life for me as a teacher was fairly easy.

Then I left teaching for a number of years to raise a family. When I began my second career in teaching in the mid-1970s, I returned with enthusiasm and big plans, only to discover that things had changed! Students seemed to be less respectful, less willing to cooperate, and certainly more vocal about what they liked and didn't like, about what they would and wouldn't do. I wasn't prepared for these changes. To complicate matters even more, my teaching assignment was in a non-traditional setting, a vocational school for students grades 11 and 12.

When I had first begun teaching in the 1950s, I'd approached each new school year with high hopes about how things would go, but also with considerable anxiety because I had only vague notions of how to translate those high hopes into reality. Though I hate to admit it, I may even have subscribed to the "Don't smile until Thanksgiving" theory. When my teaching days went smoothly, I felt lucky, and when they didn't, I felt frustrated, but I didn't know what to do about it. Now here I was, back in the same boat again, older but no wiser.

For instance, I was repeatedly caught off guard by the difference between my expectations of how students would react and how they actually reacted. The gap was huge! I was knocking myself out teaching, only to be met by stony silence and unspoken hostility, to say nothing of passive-aggressive noncompliance with almost every request or suggestion I made.

In the 1950s, in undergraduate school, methods courses had never mentioned the term "classroom management," let alone address the issue. The first encounter I had had with "real" students was in the second semester of my senior year, when I did student teaching. Luckily, student teaching had gone well then, but it ill-prepared me to deal with the problems that I was now facing daily. Back then, serious classroom-management problems were isolated incidents, not the norm, as they seemed now to be. I soon realized that the *only* place where students behaved as expected was on "The Brady Bunch" and that the only reaction I could truly count on was the unexpected one. You begin, I hope, to see the problem I was facing in my "reentry" into the profession.

That first year back was a nightmare. The speed with which I was whipping through my wonderful lesson plans caused me to have a recurring dream that I would teach everything I ever knew by October 20, and then what would I do for the rest of the year? Students were apathetic toward just about everything I planned. Forty-five-minute lesson plans were completed in twenty.

That entire first year remains a huge blur. Mercifully, I remember only bits and pieces, but one thing I *do* recall is saying to myself that if I was going to be able to survive in teaching, things would have to change drastically. And since I couldn't count on anyone or anything else changing, the changes would have to come from me. I spent that first summer after my return struggling with what I could do to make life tolerable the following school year.

I could be noble here and say that my chief motivation was to make life better for my students, and I did want that, but my main goal was my own survival and sanity. (I maintain, even now, that despite any altruistic motivations we may describe, the chief motivation for teachers making changes in their classrooms is, more than anything else, their own desperate need to survive.)

Anyway, back to my story. At that time I happened to be coaching competitive swimming, a team of six- to ten-year-olds. Practices were held outdoors. Many mornings were windy and chilly, and the water was *cold*. In order to coerce the children into water that I myself wouldn't consider entering, I initiated awards such as "Hard Worker of the Week," "Most Improved," "Most Cheerful," etc. At a little ceremony every Friday, I awarded ribbons, took Polaroid pictures, chose lane leaders for the following week, and so forth. It worked. To earn recognition, those little bodies were diving like crazy into that icy water.

I thought to myself, if these techniques work with the little ones, why wouldn't they work with older students too? Besides, what did I have to lose by trying? All they could do was laugh me out of the room. When school resumed that fall, I took the plunge with my high school juniors. I decided that unless I could get students "on my side," we would continue to lock proverbial horns.

Little by little, I began to implement rewards and incentives, and the students latched onto them in a big way. I focused on effort, behavioral, and attitudinal improvements. Since I perceive academic rolls, contests, A's on report cards, and the like to be "grand-scale" rewards, I decided instead to concentrate on strategies that would motivate students to participate in the daily activities of the classroom. I wanted to reinforce desirable behaviors and extinguish negative ones.

As I gained greater confidence, the atmosphere in my classroom changed in subtle ways. Hostility was replaced by less tension and more openness. Over time, it became increasingly less necessary for me to mentally coerce students to do my bidding. I discovered that if I let down my guard, anarchy did not spring up. Students grew less defensive.

My next goal was to convince students that they could be successful in my class. I decided that I owed it to them to foster their growth in self-discipline. If I expected them to behave appropriately and to be self-disciplined, I had to give them opportunities to demonstrate responsible behavior.

Once I was clear about that, I began to offer students choices. If they made poor ones, there were consequences, just as there were rewards when good choices were made. However, because I had no framework and no clearly defined, consistent procedures, my initiatives produced erratic results. Just as lessons require thought and structure, I soon realized that effective classroom management also requires careful planning.

That's when I came to my next realization: It is important to be proactive rather than reactive. From then on, every motivator or incentive I put into place dovetailed with what I was already doing and had a clear goal or objective attached to it, which I carefully explained to students. I even created a classroom handbook which laid out for them everything they needed to know in order to be successful in my class.

As my management system grew, I made sure that whatever I built into it met the following objectives. First, it had to *permit **and** require students to practice self-control and self-discipline*. They had to be allowed to make choices and learn to accept the consequences, both positive and negative. I frankly was tired of trying to control situations and people that were really out of my control. I decided that my role as educator wasn't to attempt to *force* students to learn or to behave appropriately, which in reality isn't possible anyway. Rather, I began to see my role as encouraging learners to make appropriate choices for themselves. Since the majority of student misbehavior is socially learned (and often reinforced), I became confident that appropriate behaviors could also be taught and learned.

Second, anything in my management plan had to be a *vital part of the instructional process.* If the sole purpose of a management plan is simply to keep students quiet and under control, of what value is it? The motivators and rewards that I decided to use had to stimulate the desire to learn.

Finally, my plan had to be a vehicle for applying rewards and incentives *systematically and consistently.* As I had learned in my earlier attempts, the occasional, random reward had little effect. Also, my intentions would have to be carefully explained to students so that they would understand the guidelines and know what to expect. I found that having a repertoire of positive, constructive techniques firmly in place was the best way to gain confidence in dealing with students. After several years of trial and error, when I had the system fairly much the way I wanted it, I named the plan Project BOOST, which stands for "Bringing Out Our Students' Talents."

So, what exactly *is* Project BOOST? It's a tightly woven plan whose single purpose is to get students to want to learn. The main element is coupons, which students essentially earn for effort and attitude, not grades. These coupons, in denominations of one, three, and five points, can be spent at any time or can be accumulated from one grading period to the next. They can be used to make purchases from a student-generated "shopping list," consisting of such items as notebook paper, suckers (which students may eat in class!), excuses from doing homework, five-minute head starts to the lunchroom or to the bus at end of the day, or a free period to study for another class. Because students generally have so little control over their lives in school, they really like having options which they can access at their pleasure. One of the most popular shopping-list items, costing fifty points, is my taking students out to lunch as my guests. Earning coupons became a terrific motivator. Some students save and horde for big-ticket items; others spend their coupons as fast as they earn them.

Another feature of Project BOOST is the Student-of-the-Week award. Individuals, selected for effort, attendance, positive attitude or another such quality, earn five-point coupons. I also take their pictures, which are posted on the Student-of-the-Week bulletin board. In addition, I mail a brief congratulatory note to their parent(s). Hardly a week passed without at least one student saying, "Tell me again what it takes to become Student-of-the Week. I'm going to be up on that bulletin board before the year's out. Just wait and see!" The motivation became so strong that I soon had to select two students per week in order to recognize all the students who deserved it.

Yet another component of Project BOOST is the "minigram." Minigrams are distributed every Monday morning and always get the week off to a pleasant start. Called "minigrams" because they're like little telegrams, they identify one or several accomplishments of students during the previous week, such as positive attitude, excellent or improved effort, or excellent or improved attendance. They are always given for goals that *all* students can attain, not just the better students, and students are not limited to the number of minigrams they can receive throughout the year.

Also, on each Monday I would announce a Class-of-the Week, recognizing one class for a collective effort such as "best attendance," "best effort on homework," or something similar. At the beginning of the school year, I take a group picture of each class. As different classes become Class-of-the-Week, I post their pictures on the same bulletin board as the Students-of-the-Week. Each member of the class receives a three-point coupon. Class-of-the-Week is a great way to make sure everyone has the opportunity to earn some coupons. Even more important, it stresses the value of cooperation and collective effort.

There are many more aspects to Project BOOST which space won't permit me to discuss here. Suffice it to say, I discovered that recognizing and rewarding those students who met expectations rather than punishing those who didn't does more than anything else to bring about positive changes in the attitudes of students and in the overall atmosphere of the classroom.

The subject of rewards raises concerns. Some teachers (*and* parents) believe that positive behavior shouldn't be rewarded. They say things like this: "Kids are *supposed* to behave! If we start to offer rewards for good behavior, what happens when they don't get rewards?" To them I say, "Think of it this way. As much as you may love your work, would you go every day just for the love of it alone? Would you go faithfully and happily if there were no paycheck or no recognition for your efforts, but merely because you're 'supposed to?' I seriously doubt it."

I'm aware of the research which says that extrinsic reinforcement won't work indefinitely, and that it is more effective with some individuals than others; that in order for changes to become permanent, *intrinsic* motivation must at some point take over. I agree. However, I also know that many students need the extrinsic motivation first in order to get them going. Inner motivation often comes later, and if it takes rewards to get them on the right path, I'm all for it.

American business and industry long ago discovered the power of praise and rewards. A study conducted in 1986 showed that U.S. companies spend more than $5 billion annually—or about $25 for every man, woman, and child in the United States—nudging their workers to sell more, produce more, or simply show up at work more often. In 1984, the Kim Lighting Company, near Los Angeles, spent nearly $200,000 on trips and prizes to reward its outdoor lighting equipment salespeople and their spouses. The Chevrolet division of General Motors spends more than $20 million a year on travel and merchandise rewards for its employees. One manufacturer not only sends his top salespeople to Hawaii but drops orchids on them from helicopters once they arrive.

Regardless of whether one believes in rewards, the fact of the matter is that they *do work.* And here's an interesting point. That same research showed that even more than the actual receiving of prizes, workers like *the process of striving to attain them;* the incentives give them something to look forward to and break up the monotony of the daily routine. I definitely found this to be true. Believe it or not, many students eagerly anticipated Monday mornings, when I would give out the minigrams and announce Students- and Class-of-the-Week.

At the same time that I was experiencing success with many students, I also had to recognize that whatever I did wouldn't work with everyone. That was hard for me to accept at first. We who become teachers are, I think, idealistic. We tend to create in our minds idealized images of what teachers are and what teaching is all about, and we knock ourselves out trying to bring those ideals to reality. Although we may not say so out loud, somewhere deep in our hearts we truly *do* believe that we really *can,* or at least *ought to* be able to, reach every child who passes through our lives, and if we don't, we've somehow failed. In the real world, of course, that's not possible. No teacher, regardless of how successful or hardworking, can reach *every* student, and that took me a while to recognize and accept.

However, Project BOOST works with most students, and I believe that it works as well as it does is because I was able somehow to convince my students, through my words and actions, that I was sincere and that I intended to deliver what I promised. A boy once told me at the end of the year that when I started talking about what all I was going to do for them with Project BOOST, he thought to himself, "Here we go again." He explained that other teachers in other years had promised rewards and incentives, but then they'd either forgotten, or gotten too busy, or had become upset and withdrawn their offers. As he spoke, I thought that perhaps he was describing me at an earlier time! He concluded with this remark: "But this time it really happened." That convinced me that it doesn't take much to get most students going. Sometimes the reward or acknowledgment might be so slight that the teacher isn't even be aware of it. A couple of occurrences convinced me of that.

First let me tell you about John. John could be a bit of a nuisance. He was sort of weird, and that tended to make him somewhat of an outcast. He also liked to tattle and get other students into trouble. Apparently he exhibited negative behavior at home as well, because it seemed that someone either at school or at home was always mad at him. I found it hard to find good things to say to and about him, but finally, one week I was able to give him a minigram.

As part of an annual autobiography assignment, I ask students to describe what has been the high point of their lives up to that time. Imagine my surprise when I read in John's autobiography that "The high point of my life so far was getting a minigram. It was the first time anyone ever told me that I could do something right. I'm going to earn more!" And he did. Now, keep in mind that John was at this time in the eleventh grade, so I seriously questioned whether no one had ever told him anything positive, but that's beside the point. For his perception, it apparently was. In John's case (as in many others'), a small thing like the minigram proved to be a behavior and attitude changer.

Another story is about Lisa. Poor Lisa was homely. There's no other way to describe her and still be at least somewhat kind. Her acne-scarred complexion and stringy hair were both the color of putty; it was hard to tell where one left off and the other started. In addition, she weighed at least three hundred pounds. Furthermore, Lisa was less than faithful about bathing. Students referred to her as "Pigpen," as well as other terms even less kind. No one, and I mean *no one*, wanted to be near her in group activities, and in all truth, I couldn't blame them. (I didn't much, either.) Talking to her about hygiene helped for a few days, but then old habits took over, and we were back where we'd started. It was not easy having Lisa in class.

Because of her excessive weight, Lisa had a hard time fitting into the table-top desks in my room. Once squeezed in, the limited space forced her rather expansive chest to rest upon the desk top. When she wore tops with scoop necklines, which seemed to be her preferred attire, we were all treated to a view of a neat, small heart tattooed at the upper edge of her left breast. Needless to say, the boys found this difficult to ignore! I tell all this only so that you'll get the full impact of the ending of this story.

Lisa's autobiography was what I would term nothing short of a horror story. She told of being given away for adoption when she was six because her parents didn't like her. She described several suicide attempts and recounted numerous times when she'd run away, once living for days under a railway bridge in downtown Columbus. She told of time spent in Rosemont, a school for incorrigible girls, and of being shifted from foster homes to institutions and back again.

As I read, I wondered whether she had made all this up to shock me or to see how I would react. I found it almost impossible to believe that anyone only sixteen could have experienced so much. However, shortly thereafter, a woman identifying herself as Lisa's social worker came to see me and, in our conversation, verified that everything in Lisa's autobiography was indeed true, plus there was even more Lisa hadn't bothered to mention!

For some reason, Lisa took a liking to me and spent lots of time in my room during her lunch hour as well as before and after school, volunteering to do small jobs for me or sitting there copying over her assignments. I was impressed that every paper she turned in to me was written in perfect penmanship. She volunteered to make notes for students who were absent and offered to write on the chalkboard for me, stating that her writing was easier to read than mine (and she got no argument there!).

At the end of each school year, I always award Perfect Attendance certificates to all students who had not missed a day of school, and in this particular year, Lisa was among them. As I handed her the certificate, she asked me whether I had looked at her school record from the previous year. I had not. She insisted that I do so. I was shocked to discover that she had missed ninety-five days! What on earth, I asked her, had made the difference between this year and last?

Imagine my amazement when she explained that during the very first week of that school year, I had praised her handwriting. (This I must have done in a casual comment because I didn't even remember doing so.) She told me that she had to come every day because I had needed her to write the notes, and she couldn't let me down! Without any awareness on my part whatsoever, Lisa had spent the entire school year focusing on ways to show off what apparently seemed to her to be her only saving grace, her handwriting. In the process she earned a consistent "B" average (her first ever) and attained perfect attendance. When presented with her certificate, she truly beamed, and even the rest of the students bestowed begrudging admiration on her.

The point is that we never know what motivates any given individual. I shudder to think how easy it might have been for Lisa or John to fall through the cracks and how little it took for them to have their share of success.

Many other teachers have found that putting a proactive classroom-management plan into action is worth the effort, as testified to by Project BOOST now being used in schools nationwide. Just as I've learned, they too have discovered that the payoffs of positive reinforcement are powerful, manifesting themselves in additional instruction time and student time-on-task. The payoffs can be seen in the gains students make in self-discipline and self-esteem or in academic achievement, positive behavior, and productive attitudes. Students learn the value of doing their best and of getting along with others, while at the same time learning to believe in themselves.

I've had much feedback from students over the years. In their final exams every year I require them to answer an essay question dealing specifically with Project BOOST, inviting them to comment both positively and negatively on the program. They are encouraged to be honest, with the assurance that they will be evaluated on how thoroughly and well they respond to the question and on how articulately they express themselves, not on whether they like or dislike the system. They are forthright and honest. Here are a few direct quotes from these essays:

> I loved having things to work for, like bonus coupons, suckers, and minigrams to take home to show my parents how good I'm doing in school.

> I've learned a lot about my self-worth and how to strive, and for this I want to thank you.

> I feel really honored to have been a Student-of-the-Week, which I think is a super idea to get students to push themselves to achieve. I was always looking forward to seeing who would get to take home minigrams, and I think it's great to be awarded coupons for trying hard in class.

> Awarding students with coupons is a very effective way to encourage students to try their best.

> I loved coming in on Monday morning to see who was Student-of-the-Week and who got the minigrams this time. It made coming to English class really fun.

My all-time favorite comment is this:

> I've never done well in English before. The rewards really encouraged me to do my best. I learned that I can do anything if I try hard enough.

I've yet to meet the teacher who can *make* anyone learn who doesn't want to. All we can do is set the tone and provide the proper environment for learning to take place. That's why I believe so strongly that effort spent on creating a positive learning environment is the best gift we can give our students. I learned this lesson as a result of my own desperation and necessity. What had started out as an ignominious beginning turned out to be a great one, and it changed not only my life in the classroom, but also that of my students.

Reference

Smith, Inga Harmon. 1993. *Discipline through Motivation: Teaching the Troops without a Whip.* Columbus, OH: Communications Unlimited.

17 To See Life Steady and Whole: Integrating the Humanities into the K–12 Curriculum

Mary Theresa Kyne
Seaton Hill College

Mary Theresa Kyne offers several key principles for making our schools places of integrative learning, where the subjects we teach, our own lives, and the lives and best learning capacities of our students can come together.

There is a fundamental question that should be carved in stone over every school entrance, to remind us all, daily, of a challenge we continually engage in. That question is "How and why should students process and integrate the information we teach?" The manner and extent to which the learner processes, assimilates, and integrates the material we present challenge us as educators in an increasingly complex world. So how do we become effective educational leaders? Every year, we try new approaches, tearing apart lesson plans and activities and re-creating them, living for those teaching moments when our students catch glimpses of how it all fits together. It is a never-ending process; it makes our profession as educational leaders challenging and keeps alive our sense of anticipation and hope.

I believe that there are five characteristics, or touchstones, common to educational leaders in a complex world in which all manner of experimentation, critical thinking, questioning, and integrating is justified, desirable, and necessary as the needs of our students and world change. Attendance to these principles, to the extent that it is possible, given our constraints and personal limitations, makes the difference between being effective leaders who integrate our subject matter with daily life, and ineffective ones who fail to show how everything in life is connected to everything else.

Seeing the Subject Matter Whole

The finest teachers I know, and the most effective student teachers I train, are passionate about the material they teach, and they know it so thoroughly that they could continue to teach it well even if every one of the classroom textbooks, teachers' guides, and latest information technologies ceased to exist. They see their subject matter at work in every facet of their own lives and in the world around them. They see the interdependence of their own discipline with all others. They see their subject whole. They are infused with it, and it is an inseparable part of their existence. "Everything connects" for these educators.

They are the history teachers who can relate the Civil War to upcoming, inevitable conflicts that have economic roots. They see the interdependence of Saudi Arabia, South Africa, and the Western world. They have a universal perspective. They can see more than the fragments and pieces. They have a window on the world through their knowledge of the past.

They are the good lecturers who draw the kernels of their best talks out of the everyday events they observe from behind their shopping sprees at the malls, or while bowling, or getting a haircut; they are "photographers" who walk through the world constantly framing shots and evaluating angles and the slant of light in order to share their insights with their students.

They are their subject matter, and for them, the inescapable linkages between their subject matter, their communities, their students, and the globe come so automatically that for them to teach otherwise—to teach a course in isolation from the world outside the classroom—would be literally and existentially impossible. Shopping lists and card games become math problems. Carpet dyes and gymnasium floor waxes become subjects of chemical analysis. The first spring flowers become topics of botanical scrutiny—and never in isolation, for each step inevitably leads to the next: that of critical thinking and questioning. Why and how do these spring flowers acquire color and fragrance? Of what are they composed? Why do people write poems about flowers? What have they written of them down through the ages? Why do people give flowers to each other? Do the colors of the flowers they give mean anything? Why? How can we plant a Shakespearean garden? Why should we? What do environmental scientists do? How can we help our students to realize the difference they can make in the professions of ecology, environmental science, the scientific fields, the humanities?

In *School and Society,* first published in 1899, John Dewey wrote that

> From the standpoint of the child, the great waste in school comes from his inability to utilize the experiences he gets outside of school in any complete and free way while, on the other hand, he is unable to apply in daily life what he is learning at school.

We're here to help our students open a window on adulthood, on the essentials of their lives; we help by opening our curricula to the pre-occupations, perspectives, and growing pains of young people. They're more likely to learn in the presence of cooperative and knowledgeable teachers who are convinced of the value of their subjects and enthusiastic about sharing what they know.

Without dictating methods of integrating the humanities in your curriculum, I'd like to share with you seven principles that seem to me to be at the foundation of integrating subject matter and life:

1. Students need to read and write about their curricular and extracurricular lives. They need regular blocks of time—time to think, write, confer, read, change their minds, and write some more. They need time they can count on, so that even when they aren't writing or reading, they're anticipating the time when they will be. They simply need time to read and write well. It is our responsibility to provide such an environment.

2. Students need their own topics. From the first day of kindergarten, they should view writing as a way to think about and give voice to their own ideas and concerns. We need to balance assigned topics with free themes, but those which meet the objectives we're teaching. For example, you can assign students to become a literary or historical *persona* about whom you've been studying and have them write journal accounts from that character's perspective. In doing this, you could provide certain questions to which they will respond, while you free their spirit to write in a different, more empathic voice. They will become more attuned to the motivations and drives of the characters about whom they are reading and studying and will personalize the subject matter, since it will now have a direct bearing on their written work.

3. Students need response. Helpful response comes during—not after—the composing process. It should come from the writer's peers as well as from the teacher, who consistently suggests restatements and

questions that help writers reflect on the content of their writing in journals, poems, stories, and reflective papers, as well as in essays and formal papers.

4. Students learn mechanics in context from peers and teachers who address errors as they occur within individual pieces of writing, wherein these rules and forms will have meaning and purpose. We must listen to the educators who tell us that it is a mistake to suppose that instruction in grammar transfers readily to the actual uses of language. Research suggests that the finer points of writing, such as punctuation and subject-verb agreement, are best learned while students are engaged in extended writing that has the purpose of communicating a message to an audience. No communicative purpose is served when children are asked merely to identify the parts of speech on a worksheet. Effective teachers find ways to give children reasons to communicate to real audiences. Lady Macbeth, for example, wouldn't want her journal to reveal a "weak, lily-livered" writer! As teachers, we can sometimes grade papers collaboratively, a science teacher grading a set of term papers for scientific content and a friend in the English department grading them for grammar and compositional style.

5. Students need to see our writing. We need to demonstrate what experienced writers do in the process of composing, letting our students see our own drafts and the folios of Shakespeare and other famous authors in all their messiness and tentativeness.

6. Students need to read. They need access to a wide variety of texts, plays, prose and poetry, biography, autobiography, satire, mathematical and scientific journals and magazines, and the daily newspaper.

7. Students need structure that keeps them on track and allows them to be creative. Teach your students the meaning of Gustave Flaubert's philosophy: "Be regular and ordinary in your life like a bourgeois so that you may be violent and original in your work."

The first step, then, is to examine again our methodology of what clearly works and what doesn't. Through the humanities, students can find solace and inspiration, and a means by which—even if they are unpopular or shy or disabled—they can communicate with others and form friendships. Through the humanities, the chance exists that their sensitivity to themselves and others can be nourished and kept alive. Businesses and corporations want creative employees who have the ability to study a problem, see it whole in all its parts, and with imagination, propose a workable solution. The historian Arthur Schlesinger Jr. says that "creativity implies the ability on the part of the creator to carry others with him in the endless quest for insight." Handled properly, the humanities become the means by which our students' emotions can be gathered into focused beams of light and energy.

Knowing How Learning Takes Place

Effective educational leaders are convinced that all young people can learn, and this conviction is at the heart of our philosophy of education.

The capacity for learning and integrating experiences is innate. Human beings constantly process data and information. Indeed, it is as natural to learn as it is to breathe. Two of the most complex skills of all are learned without formal education: walking upright and talking. In his *Aims of Education* (first published in 1929), Alfred North Whitehead wrote:

> The first intellectual task which confronts an infant is the acquirement of spoken language. What an appalling task, the correlation of meanings with sounds! It requires an analysis of ideas and an analysis of sounds. We all know that the infant does it, and that the miracle of his achievement is inexplicable. But so are all miracles, and yet to the wise they remain miracles. All I ask is that with this example staring us in the face we should cease talking nonsense about postponing the harder subjects. (16)

In too many instances, students just don't know what we or our textbooks are talking about, or they cannot make any connection between that information and their world. Therefore, they cannot internalize the information or make use of it, and so it's discarded as irrelevant as soon as the tests are taken.

In today's society, unlike previous ones, young people's lives are centered on their jobs, technology, television, and video machines. We need to show them how to place these experiences into a context in which they can be tested and applied to their academic and personal lives. For example, viewing life as a journey similar to the one undertaken by Chaucer's pilgrims is wonderfully appropriate for our mall-ers! Let them create contemporary pilgrims and describe them, if not in iambic pentameter, then at least in decameter! Have them accompany the description with an artistic rendition of a favorite pilgrim, either Chaucerian or contemporary. Allow them to personalize the literature. The need for memorization, attention to detail, and dexterity that is so vital to creating and running a computer program is just as vital to an understanding of *how* and *what* a poem or an artistic piece means. Both have validity and merit; both command our respect; both are integral to their lives. As children grow and their questions and ability to understand and apply what they learn becomes increasingly complex, their need for this integrative experience also grows.

Likewise, when you as teacher try out ideas *with* your students and you work side by side, letting them figure out things for themselves but gently guiding their approaches, the amount of learning and confidence increases far more than it would if you repeatedly gave them explicit instructions and lecture notes.

This whole matter of meaningful experience and its relation to our subject matter is a tremendously important one in our curriculum. Obviously, there has to be a balance between teaching only by lectures and text and teaching only by direct experience. I challenge us to ask this question each time we prepare lesson plans: How and why should my students process and integrate the information I'm planning to teach?

Knowing the Students and Their Environments

When we know students reasonably well, we know the extent of the demands we can make upon them, how much we can engage their cooperation in the learning process, their talents, abilities, likes, and dislikes. We know the kind of constructive criticism they will respond to and not be crushed or repelled by. We know something about their readiness to accept responsibility, and in what amounts. And our students know us.

To continue to make our educational system integrative and effective, we must start with the real-world reality of our students' lives, be it centered on McDonald's, a farm, or a ghetto street—accept that, build on that, and broaden that. Otherwise, we demean that reality or negate it. We imply that nothing they've learned in the experiential area of their lives is valid or relevant. We deny their heritage and their present and proceed from the assumption that they're deprived and that we must correct the situation quickly.

To bring our education and their lives together takes time, a willingness to know our students better, a sensitivity about the way we approach them, and an opportunity to have them articulate and own their environments. When a working relationship evolves, we see each other in a completely new light and respect each other far more.

Then we can introduce them to the new world of the past, challenge them to new heights of discovery, and encourage their inherent potential to become holistic, life-long learners.

Being Careful about Assumptions Concerning the Students

The prophecy of self-fulfillment allows us three things: to be honestly attentive to what is really going on in the classroom so that we're not just wishing for good results unrealistically; not to believe others' assumptions about our students; and not to trust our own assumptions, especially if they're negative and not based on facts. This is where getting to know students better plays such an important role, for too often the so-called "facts" upon which we base our assumptions and approaches are misleading. Test scores, quality of homework, classroom performance, and behavior, as we know, are not the best indicators of potential or ability.

John J. Mitchell, in his book *The Adolescent Predicament*, states that "All healthy humans, universally and without fail, abhor not making a difference. It is the closest thing to nonexistence [that humans] can experience" (Mitchell 1975, 55). Evidence shows not only that young people are hungry to—and can—make such a difference, but also that to deny them the opportunity cripples them, or forces them to strive to make that difference illegally or in ways that we cannot accept. The basic skills and the outcomes-based education that we hear so much about lately will only be superficially mastered if the sole motivations we can offer students are extrinsic. They must be inextricably wedded with their psychological preparedness: their need for self-esteem and confidence. We have to watch constantly for such opportunities and take advantage of them, knowing that we're making a difference, and knowing that we're turning around completely negative, defeatist attitudes about self and potential. I strongly believe that what I do as a teacher is important. As Hugh Kenner said in a recent issue of *Johns Hopkins Magazine*: "Someone's life may be changed by a suggestion you never meant to implant, by a casual word. . . . What we do as teachers matters. And what we do, therefore, deserves all the attention we can muster."

As always, we need to strike a balance. Students know when they've given an assignment an honest attempt and merit a justified compliment, and when only their halfhearted efforts result in over-praise or false praise.

Helping Students Analyze and Respond Appropriately to Situations

Because we're about the business of educating the total person, we must be concerned about student development in all its aspects. That means going beyond the content of many of our courses and helping students integrate their lives with the kinds of adults they will eventually be. And that means not only scrutinizing the example we ourselves set as individuals, but also helping them interpret accurately and respond appropriately to the situations that arise. We enable our students to make ethical judgments as we debate, for example, about the characterization, theme, or plot of a literary story or a theatrical production.

In class, I like to initiate this process, encouraging students to challenge my opinions, sometimes interspersing my remarks with obviously unworkable or unpopular stances to provoke discussion and argument and to give them some exercise in this type of thinking.

Our schools are fine and essential places to begin building that knowledge and resolve, for there students can be trained early in the company of sensitive adults to act appropriately and wisely—to integrate their brains and their consciences—not only in terms of the increased motivation that occurs as academic skills are learned, but also in terms of personal growth, self-confidence, and integrity.

School and life can come alive in practical, vigorous ways. We create a healing and holistic space when we make the classroom an environment wherein young minds can work and play safely and steadily. Our teaching profession is a rebirth, a chance to start anew. At the end of our careers, we want to say, "My students, I leave you happy. Life has been mine. I hold you in my heart and find you good."

References

Atwell, Nancie. 1987. *In the Middle: Writing, Reading, and Learning with Adolescents.* Upper Montclair, NJ: Boynton/Cook.

Dewey, John. [1899] 1900. *School and Society.* Chicago: University of Chicago Press.

Mitchell, John J. 1975. *The Adolescent Predicament.* Toronto: Holt, Rinehart & Winston.

Whitehead, Alfred North. [1929] 1967. *The Aims of Education and Other Essays.* New York: Macmillan.

18 Questions, Confusions, and Resolutions of a First-Year Teacher

Richard F. Gaspar
Van Buren Junior High School, Tampa, Florida

Richard F. Gaspar offers practical, pragmatic advice to new teachers about the importance of a supportive administration and colleagues and, above all, of being organized and patient.

As dawn breaks on my classroom, I stand under the sign reading "Mr. Gaspar's Neighborhood" and gaze over the thirty-five young and restless faces gleaming back at me. The first golden day of school has arrived, and I nervously ponder the many questions flying through my head. "How am I going to get all of these students into thirty desks?" "Where is the staff bathroom located?" "How can I ask 6'4" Gilbert not to sit in front of 4'11" Nora after I have just told him to sit wherever he would like?" These are just a few of the challenges that arose to disrupt my "great beginning." Yet, soon the bell rang, and then another, and so on, and before I knew it I had survived my first day as a paid intern and English and reading teacher in the Alternative Education program at Pasco Comprehensive High School. When I think back over my preparation for that day, I realize that four elements contributed greatly to my success: a supportive and involved administration, a warm and friendly peer teacher, being extremely organized, and having a pocket full of unending patience.

Fortunately, my first year as a teacher occurred at a school where the administration is actively involved with teachers and teacher preparation. Repeatedly, the principal and vice-principals took their time to answer my questions and clarify my confusions. Equally important, the administration provided the entire staff with a week-long orientation to ensure that everyone was prepared and ready for the first day of school. This was particularly helpful for me, as it allowed me the time to meet all of my peers and to become comfortable with the school and its surroundings. Even though the seventy-eight-acre campus keeps the administrators busy, they make sure they find the time to provide teachers with assistance and resolutions.

Likewise, the administration is always available when I need classroom assistance. Although many people view administrators as disciplinarians, this is not necessarily their only role. From assisting me in choral reading activities in class, to providing me with the opportunity to attend conferences and inservices, they try to accommodate almost any request—and this is extremely important in developing the confidence of a first-year teacher. By being there for me to lean on, they have helped me to stand firmer as a teacher and a leader.

Undoubtedly, the greatest asset to my great beginning was my peer teacher. Although her official duties obligated her to "assist the beginning teacher in the Professional Orientation program," she did far more. Throughout the day she provided me with hugs, help, and visits, when they were most needed. From clarifying the pronunciation of "Jaurequi" and "Jaramillo" to tips on effective classroom management, she prepared me for well beyond the first day of school. For this reason, I am extremely comfortable with asking my peers for advice, resources, and assistance, whenever the need arises. Even though the English teacher in Room 604 sponsors cheerleading, yearbook, journalism, and leads the testing committee, she always places people as her first priority. Whether they are students, staff, or parents, everyone finds a friend in my peer teacher.

Truly, a peer teacher is an absolute necessity for understanding and balancing the duties of a first-year teacher. A peer can provide insight in communicating with parents and also provide a new teacher with an understanding of the community the school serves. A good peer teacher lets his or her duties go beyond the school day, encompassing all of the areas of the educational environment.

One necessity a beginning teacher must possess is good organization. I made sure that as students walked into my room on the first day of school, they were welcomed by an orderly and neatly decorated environment. Every aspect of a teacher's day requires order. From scheduling classes and lesson plans to meeting with parents, the more a teacher plans out a school day, the smoother it will progress. When I finally learned what "lunch duty" entailed and all the responsibilities that "club sponsorship" required, I was comforted that my school day was organized.

All in all, organization keeps the entire school running efficiently. Before the first day arrives a teacher should understand both daily and emergency procedures. It is also imperative that the students be equally familiar with school plans within the first few days of school. By posting procedures and evacuation routes in easy-to-view places in the room, a teacher can ensure the safety and security of his or her students.

Likewise, by ensuring that your lesson plans, classroom procedures, and classroom management follow a logical pattern, a first-year teacher can begin the first day of school feeling comfortable and confident.

Equally important to having a good administration, peer teacher, and organization is having patience. Not every student comes to school each day ready to learn and thrive. Some students come to school hungry and tired, and their parents never ask: "What did you learn in school today?" Patience is not a virtue, but a *necessity*. When I am frustrated, thinking about how difficult some things have been for me to understand often helps me realize the confusion a student is experiencing. Although as a teacher it is difficult for me to see the importance of discussing "Beavis and Butthead" during a vocabulary lesson, patience allows me to handle the situation appropriately.

Put another way, not every school day will go smoothly. Maybe the song title "If Today Was a Fish, I'd Throw It Back In" best expresses why teachers need patience. Students aren't fish, and as teachers we must see them all as "keepers." By being patient we can model for students how to achieve progress as well as save ourselves from unmanageable stress. Sometimes it can be difficult not seeing one student as a "wide-mouthed bass" and another as a "rouge shark," but inside each of them is a student waiting to be reached. Parents see their children as jewels and treasures, and with patience, so can we. Much like Hemingway's resolute fisher, we must use our patience to conquer difficulties.

All teachers deserve to have a "great beginning." Of course, we must also realize that they don't happen by themselves. Administrators must ensure that new teachers are familiar and comfortable with both their peers and their environment. Additionally, administrators can provide invaluable assistance in the classroom. Equally important is the role a peer teacher plays in the development of a new teacher. A good peer teacher can make the difference in a great or horrific first year. In the same way, a teacher can ensure a great beginning by being patient and organized.

In short, a great beginning is more than surviving from dawn to dusk each day. It is realizing that "Nothing Gold Can Stay." Therefore, every teacher must understand that not every day will be bright and sunny. Yet, as educators we must see the gold inside each student and polish it until it shines from within. We must try to show students the way to discover their hidden treasures and how to organize themselves to be successful. By doing this, we create the possibility that someday each student will go home and say, "Wait till I tell you what I learned in school today!"

19 Teaching Is All I Know on Earth, and All I Need to Know

Gerald Mackey
Trident Technical College

Drawing on twenty years of varied experience as an educator, Gerald Mackey offers new teachers a concise but comprehensive set of "survival tips" that have helped him to feel that teaching is truly his life.

During the past twenty years, I have worked as a high school teacher, a teacher evaluator, a principal, and more recently as a college professor. My experience as a teacher evaluator and a school administrator has taken me in and out of hundreds of classrooms, all subjects and all grade levels. Too often, I see first-year teachers with great potential throw up their hands and quit out of frustration. After four years of diligent preparation for a career in teaching, this should not be the case.

The first year is the most critical year in a teacher's career. Hence, administrators should provide as much assistance and support as possible to help teachers succeed. Beginning teachers, on the other hand, can also help themselves by implementing the following simple, but practical, survival tips. Some of these lessons were learned early on in my career, and others came several years later through trial and error.

1. *Plan effective, meaningful activities for the entire day—every day.* Bell-to-bell planning and academic-engaged time should be the order of the day. Too many teachers make the mistake of planning a fifteen- or twenty-minute lesson for a fifty-minute class period. Discipline problems and, in some cases today, mayhem, often occur when students sit idly waiting for others to complete an assignment or when they have nothing to do. The key here is to *overplan*, if there is such a thing. Should you finish the lesson in question ahead of time, move on with the next day's lesson. But by no means should students be allowed to use valuable instructional time for socializing.

2. *Organize and have at hand all instructional materials and equipment for each class and subject ahead of time.* Be prepared to start the lesson at the ringing of the bell. Research shows that the first few minutes of the class period are the most critical. You should not have to search for materials or set up equipment once class starts. Also, do not waste instructional time on "administrivia" (clerical tasks). Madeline Hunter (1982), the renowned educator, psychologist, and guru of the Program for Effective Teaching (PET) model, suggests involving students in some meaningful learning activities, if housekeeping chores must be done at the beginning of the lesson (25–30). A math teacher, for example, may have two or three problems on the board for students to solve. An English teacher discussing action verbs may ask students to make a list of action verbs which show all of the actions they were involved in prior to coming to school. This technique is effective in any discipline, and the creativity it allows is unbelievable.

3. *Teach! Do not allow independent and worksheet activities to take the place of direct hard-core instruction.* Just as you must plan bell-to-bell instruction, you must also teach all day, every day. Too often we assign activities to students without giving them the essentials that they need to complete the assigned tasks. Be sure to provide lots of explanations, definitions, examples, and illustrations. If a process is required, model the process first. Monitor student progress and understanding at appropriate points in the lesson. Use worksheet activities only to reinforce or assess skills that have been thoroughly taught.

4. *Don't be a slave to the teacher's manual.* Marva Collins (1991), the founder and president of the nationally acclaimed Westside Preparatory School in Chicago, Illinois, says that we must make learning "come alive" (38). In order to do this, says Collins, we must remove ourselves from "prepackaged lesson plans" (39). If you do not feel confident using your own creative ideas at first, study and learn what is in the manual so that you will be able to communicate these ideas with confidence and authority. You can gradually work in some of your own ideas as your level of confidence increases. Students are quite perceptive, and they know when a teacher knows his or her subject matter or is faking it. Hence, you don't want students to see that you are obviously dependent on the teacher's manual.

5. *Develop a classroom-management plan which clearly outlines classroom rules and expectations and the consequences for each infraction.*

Classroom discipline is crucial to effective teaching; no learning takes place in a noisy, disruptive environment. Discuss the management plan with students and post the plan in a conspicuous location in the classroom. You should also send the plan home for parents' signatures, indicating that they have read and understand the plan and have discussed it with their child. Remind students of the plan when the need arises, but above all, be fair, be firm, and be consistent.

6. *Involve parents early on.* An amicable partnership should exist between the school and the home. Everyone must work together in the best interests of the child. Don't be afraid to call parents at home or to invite parents in for a conference when there is a concern, or just to discuss the student's progress. Parental involvement, as many studies[1] show, translates into academic and social success for students. Communication with parents, then, should be ongoing and not only when the student is having an academic or social problem. When you catch students being good, certainly you want to reinforce and reward this behavior by communicating it to parents. A simple note (or whatever creative techniques you have devised) will do. One of the best practical sources that I have used and found to be extremely effective in involving and communicating with parents is Lee Canter's *Parent Conference Book* (1984). This book is a guaranteed formula for success, and I strongly recommend it for beginning teachers.

7. *Learn as much as you can about your students as quickly as possible.* First, learn their names. This feat can easily be accomplished by devising a seating chart during the first few days of class. Addressing students by name also helps with discipline problems. Students are often mischievous when they think that a teacher does not know their name. Surprise them and notice the facial expression when you call the name of a student who least expects you to know his or her name. Also, learn the ability levels, the learning styles, and any other pertinent data concerning your students so that you will be able to plan instruction accordingly.

8. *Keep abreast of current trends in your content area.* If I were forced to attribute my success in teaching to a single-most factor, this survival tip would be it. To this day, twenty years after totally immersing myself in professional development activities, I've yet to come up for air. A reservoir of learning resources awaits you; all you need to do is tap into the source. Subscribe to and read your

content-area journal; join professional organizations; and attend work-shops, conventions, seminars, and inservice programs. These sessions will help you to grow professionally and provide you with opportu-nities to network with others both in and outside of your discipline. You will be amazed at the number of practical and successful teaching ideas that you will get from networking with peers. Also, take advan-tage of all those free summer educational perks, especially studying abroad, offered by colleges and universities, institutes, the National Endowment for the Humanities, and the like. No amount of classroom theories can begin to equal the benefits that come from interacting and sharing with others.

9. *When in doubt, seek help from experienced colleagues and adminis-trators.* Many principals now provide a buddy teacher or mentor for beginning teachers. Make use of this amenity. Don't feel that you must operate in a vacuum. If you are not clear on a particular policy or pro-cedure, seek help from your administrator or one of your experienced colleagues. The same holds true if you need help with lesson plans, discipline problems, or any number of situations a beginning teacher may encounter. View your attempt to get help not as a sign of weak-ness or incompetence, but as an opportunity to mature professionally. You need not feel guilty—even the most experienced of us are still picking one another's brain.

10. *Be human. Allow for mistakes and acknowledge them as arches to build upon.* Don't feel that you must know everything or have all of the answers. Students will appreciate you for it. Marva Collins, for example, tells of how one of her fourth graders called her atten-tion to a quotation in her book *The Marva Collins Story* that she erro-neously attributed to Aesop instead of its original source, la Fontaine. To the student's correction, Collins says, "[I]t shows that they are paying attention, that they are in school for the right reason. . . . [I]t shows that they are thinking" (1991, 37). One of the joys of teaching is having those vigilant, astute minds keep us in check, and we should encourage more of it. Like our students, we can also learn from our mistakes, whether those mistakes are pro-cedural or content related.

11. *Show enthusiasm for what you are doing.* As you have often heard, enthusiasm breeds enthusiasm. Students can tell whether you enjoy what you are doing. Believe me, they watch our every move—even moves that we ourselves are not aware of. Just recently, for exam-

ple, I got my "Student Evaluation of Course and Instructor" results from my department head and was certainly moved by some of the comments the students made concerning my enthusiasm for the course:

> He is full of too much energy so early in the morning.
>
> He's entertaining and helpful.
>
> He is also very enthusiastic and a positive thinker.
>
> He enjoys his work and it shows by the way he teaches.
>
> His classes are alive and interesting.
>
> If all instructors taught with the same love . . .

The list goes on and suggests that as teachers, we are always on stage. So be an actor or actress. Let yourself go! The worst thing that could happen is that you'll have a captive audience, highly motivated and on fire for learning.

12. *Maintain a sense of humor at all costs.* Don't take every comment or action of a student as a personal attack on you. The adage of not smiling until Christmas or after no longer works. Learn to laugh at yourself and with your students. Laughter relieves stress and tension for both you and the students. Humor, though, should never be at the expense of the students.

Teaching is a noble profession. In fact, teaching is my life. Even in my role as an evaluator and a principal, I found myself teaching students and teaching teachers how to teach. I often explore mentally which other professions would offer me the personal satisfaction and fulfillment that I get from teaching, but the search, not surprisingly, always yields none. If you follow these simple tips and the others delineated here in *Great Beginnings*, you, too, will look back twenty years from now, I am sure, and find yourself paraphrasing the immortal words of John Keats in "Ode on a Grecian Urn": "Teaching is all I know on earth, and all I need to know." Good luck!

Note

1. See, for example, Keith et al. (1986).

References

Canter, Lee. 1984. *Parent Conference Book.* Santa Monica: Canter and Associates.

Collins, Marva N. 1991. "Relighting the Candles of Excellence across America." *Vital Issues: The Journal of African American Speeches* 1: 30–39.

Hunter, Madeline C. 1982. *Mastery Teaching.* El Segundo, CA: TIP.

Keith, Timothy, et al. 1986. "Parental Involvement, Homework, and TV Time: Direct and Indirect Effects on High School Achievement." *Journal of Educational Psychology* 78.5 (Oct.): 373–80.

III For the English Leader

Recalling their own early days in the classroom, and recognizing the difficult negotiation that must often take place between support for new teachers and productive criticism, the eight experienced English department chairs and three experienced chairs in this section offer practical and immediately usable suggestions—including finding a language for teacher evaluation, developing programs to bridge pre-service and inservice training, and using storytelling, journal writing, and teaching portfolios—for supporting new teachers as they become increasingly skilled and reflective in their work as educators.

20 Three New Teachers in the English Department

Jane E. Harvey, Daniel A. Heller, Jennifer S. McConnell, and Debra J. Williams
Brattleboro Union High School, Brattleboro, Vermont

Three teachers new to one high school English department and the department chair note the concerns that they raised in their discussions, negotiating the delicate balance between supportive and intrusive supervision and emphasizing above all the importance of, as one of them writes, "TLC."

In the spring of 1992, Brattleboro Union High School found itself with the rare opportunity of being able to hire three new English teachers. While the three hired were not exactly new teachers, they were new to the school. Jane Harvey had been a long-term substitute for the previous three years in Connecticut. Jennifer McConnell had taught for three years before coming to Brattleboro. Debra Williams was a seven-year veteran, returning from Colorado to teach here, in the high school from which she graduated. Dan Heller, English Department head since 1989, had taught for eighteen years, sixteen of them at BUHS.

These four professionals spent a morning sharing their perspectives on the lives of new teachers, from both the administrative and teaching points of view. Following this exchange, they each wrote down individual thoughts, which have been compiled for this article.

Jennifer focused immediately on the supervisory role, noting that it cut in two directions. "It may help to remember that, not only did you interview and hire new teachers, they interviewed you to see if you would provide an environment conducive to personal and professional growth," she wrote. The relationship between supervisor and new teacher is a delicate and crucial one. Each individual reacts differently to being observed, to having his or her work critiqued. Debra felt, "I like the idea of multiple observations during the first year. This allows the new teacher to become more comfortable with the idea of having an observer/evaluator/supervisor in the class-room." Jane suggested "a few unofficial observations before the recorded ones," to get the new teacher used to the process.

Everyone agreed on the value of preconferences, both before specific observations and at the opening of school, to set up the process for the entire year. On the other hand, Dan saw the value in some combination of announced and unannounced observations. In this way, he said, "I can get a better picture of the teacher's strengths and weaknesses. Sure, a teacher should be allowed to invite the supervisor in to see her best work, but there is also the day-to-day work to examine."

The way supervisor and teacher conduct visitation and evaluation is also important. Jennifer wrote, "A crucial time for this new partnership is after the final interview but before the first week of school. . . . Once the contract has been signed, the direct supervisor should contact the new teacher to arrange a meeting so that concerns about curriculum, supervision, and the building can be addressed." Both Jennifer and Debra saw the value in a common language of supervision. All administrators and a number of teachers in this district have taken a course in teaching strategies which helps to define our supervision and evaluation work. For Debra, "It was very helpful to me to take a course similar to one my supervisor took; it helps me to understand his observations better, and I think it will improve communication between us about these observations." In Jennifer's opinion, "Every school district should adopt a specific model of supervision. At the very least there needs to be a common language." Yet, the supervisor must be careful not to overwhelm the new teacher. As Jane put it, "Too much support is unwelcome. I tend to feel strangled, resentful, not trusted if there is a constant presence of a watchful eye. Let me find my own way, but give me the resources to seek out information."

For Dan, this is a tough call. The contract demands that each teacher new to the district be formally observed at least four times by the middle of March. As he sees it,

> The crucial factor is to establish trust. You have to convince the new teacher that you are not going to pull the rug out, that the criticisms you raise are not punitive but growth oriented. If I say that students were not actively involved in the lesson, my purpose is to then engage in a dialogue with the teacher for developing strategies to make students more active learners, not to document flaws for an ultimate summative review.

If teacher and supervisor trust each other, a rich professional dialogue, useful to both of them, can develop.

One strategy the supervisor can employ to help new teachers is to provide information. Here again, a delicate balance exists between providing the necessary information and overwhelming the new teacher with too much. As Jane put it, "The biggest problem, I think, was not a lack of support, but a lack of information." All three new teachers focused on this need for information, on various levels and in various areas.

"If your school district does not already have one, create a manual that describes the school, including all its policies, procedures, and little-known facts. . . . Perhaps a second-year teacher could be enlisted to help. What did that person learn the hard way and what would they say to a new hire?" This suggestion by Jennifer was echoed by Debra: "I feel like the biggest problem I've faced as a new teacher here is a lack of communication from the administration relating to nonteaching areas. For example, I was assigned hall duty, but was never told exactly what that entailed." Jane spoke to the balance between too much and not enough. "Rather than explaining all procedures at the beginning, supply information and assistance when a procedure is needed, for example, at the time when teachers are to write progress reports."

One strategy we used in the English Department at Brattleboro Union High School was assigning new teachers to experienced department members as mentors. Debra's thoughts on this were as follows:

> I liked very much the idea of having a peer mentor. I was very nervous about starting this job, where the only teachers I would know were ones I had had as a student here. It was incredibly comforting to receive a letter from a fellow English teacher, welcoming me to the school community and encouraging me to contact her if I had any questions or needed help in any areas. I didn't feel the need to contact her before school started, but once the school year began I turned to her a lot for advice and information on little things, like what had to be done before taking a course, how to request a day off, etc. She was very helpful, both in the practical aspects and in making me feel more comfortable as a new teacher here.

Jane appreciated "having another new teacher as a 'roommate' " (we have a space problem) and "being assigned a department buddy."

According to Dan, the very culture of the school has a profound effect on the integration of new people. The English Department has consciously worked on developing an atmosphere of supportive peer relationships. This environment came through for these new teachers.

Jane described her English colleagues as "a supportive, open, friendly, generous department." Debra mentioned that

> another thing that the English Department has done throughout the year to help me is to be willing to share any and all materials pertaining to areas that I was going to be teaching but with which I did not feel entirely comfortable. For example, when I mentioned to a couple of teachers that I needed to teach *The Great Gatsby* to my junior class and I had never taught it before, both of them immediately offered me all the materials that they had on that work, and also spent a great deal of time talking to me about the book and ways to present it to students.

Jane suggested that new teachers be given "a list of department members and the classes they teach and their areas of specialization."

"In some ways, what makes the job of the new teacher easier are the intangibles," said Dan. "If there is an atmosphere, a culture of acceptance and cooperation, the new teacher will feel at home more readily." Jennifer suggested that "in addition to helping them locate community services in order to feel at home, it is helpful to introduce them to faculty in an out-of-school setting. Have a cookout for new faculty." She recalled the colleagues at her first school, which was in a rural area: "They opened their homes and families to young teachers who were far away from their families and who could not afford to fly home for the holidays." Debra mentioned that

> It would be nice if, during the first working days, colleagues made the effort to include new teachers in their plans for lunch. And once school has started with students present, such little things as being invited to join a table in the faculty room for lunch can make a big difference in making a new teacher feel comfortable and part of things. It would be great if everyone in the school really made an effort at the very start of the school year to include new teachers in every aspect of the social life of the school.

A wonderful suggestion of Jennifer's was to give the new teacher a copy of the school yearbook so he or she could begin to learn names and positions. And along the lines of lunch, she said, "Nothing will make a person feel more welcomed than to have four invitations to lunch."

All three teachers addressed the issue of class assignments. Clearly, the consensus was not to give the "bad" classes to the new person. As Jennifer put it,

> Nothing will cause burn-out in a new teacher quicker than giving him or her all freshmen, or all remedial, or all discipline problems. If anything, these new teachers need time to test their new

wings, to try out their knowledge in an elective area. They bring with them freshness and enthusiasm straight from the world of academe. Tap into their resources—do not let them go to waste.

Dan agreed. "It has always been my policy, with veteran as well as new teachers, to share the wealth and the problems, and that includes me. If you think about it, the best teachers should get the most difficult classes, not teachers who are inexperienced." Trial by fire or paying one's dues is not a positive or productive way to introduce new people to an institution or the profession. Debra appreciated having course outlines to work from. "Believe it or not," she said, "When I took my first job, I was not given anything like that, no curriculum guide, nothing; in fact, I had to ask for a list of books that would be used in the classes I would be teaching. As a brand new, just-out-of-college teacher, I was definitely lost."

The new teacher, experienced or not, is an individual, a human being with needs, concerns, fears. A supervisor can do much to ease the transition into a new position for this person, as can a department. However, our discussions pointed to the need for a systemic approach to new members of the school, a culture of openness, professionalism, friendliness, patience, and caring. "You cannot completely buffer the ride for a new teacher," said Jennifer. "Teaching is a demanding and rewarding profession. You can, however, take some concrete measures to help make the transition from student teacher to full-time faculty member a time for personal and professional growth," Debra added, "New teachers are intelligent, creative, and resourceful, but they're not mind readers or magicians; a little guidance, information sharing, and (corny as it may sound) TLC can make a big difference in the way we feel about our new schools."

21 A Storytelling Approach to Beginning Teacher Evaluation

Thomas Philion
University of Illinois at Chicago

Thomas Philion suggests that the deep-seated desire for narrative, for reading and writing stories, that "inspired most of us . . . to become English teachers in the first place" can be a powerful way of turning the evaluation of newer teachers into an opportunity for shared reflection and inquiry.

How should mentor teachers evaluate beginning English teachers? Over the past two years, I have reflected upon this question numerous times in the context of supervising student teachers in the Secondary English Teacher Education program at the University of Illinois at Chicago. The answer that I have developed is both sensible and difficult to understand: write stories.

I advocate storytelling as a method of evaluation because I believe that formal processes of observation and evaluation ought to facilitate professional growth and development. Writing stories about lessons conducted by beginning English teachers encourages professional growth and development in two important and unique ways. First, storytelling fosters the comfortable but yet challenging social environment in which beginning English teachers can learn. Second, in stories, mentor teachers can embed the kind of useful information that enables pedagogical reflection and inquiry.

My notion that storytelling fosters the comfortable but yet challenging social environment in which beginning English teachers can learn is derived in part from my reading of *Talented Teenagers: The Roots of Success and Failure* (1993). In *Talented Teenagers*, Mihalyi Csikszentmihalyi and his colleagues Kevin Rathunde and Samuel Whalen argue that people learn when they enjoy the activities in which they engage (8). Additionally, they propose that the social environments that support learning are both comfortable and challenging in nature (15). If there is one thing that I know about beginning English teachers, it is that they love a good story. When mentor teachers write descriptive and personal accounts of lessons that they have observed, they tap into this passion. They create a situation where beginning English teachers feel comfortable, but challenged, too.

If beginning English teachers feel challenged by stories about their teaching, they feel this way because there is so much rich and useful—and sometimes even embarrassing—detail contained in personal narratives. As Robert Coles explains in *The Call of Stories: Teaching and the Moral Imagination* (1989), stories provide insights into human relations that traditional research cannot supply. Coles's view parallels that of a growing number of educational researchers who argue that descriptive accounts of classroom practice furnish teachers with essential information about teaching (Goswami and Stillman 1987; Atwell 1987; Cochran-Smith and Lytle 1993). According to these researchers, storytelling enables reflection upon the personal and emotional aspects of teaching. Furthermore, it facilitates inquiry into the social conditions that support learning.

How does one write a storytelling evaluation? This is how I started a recent account of a formal observation of a beginning English teacher:

> At the beginning of 5th period, I walk into the classroom in which Stephanie is student teaching. As usual, I arrive just before the bell rings and find my seat in the back of the room. This is a class that I have observed twice now. Students sit in straight rows and there are about 13 students. Posters advertising young adult literature from the 1970s cover the far windows. The boys who find seats in the back of the class enter roughly. They aren't ready to jump into the pleasures of reading. A dusty and empty black steel bookrack sits between myself and these boys.

Typically, I approach the writing of a storytelling evaluation from the perspective of an ethnographer or cultural anthropologist.[1] I highlight physical detail, and I record discursive interactions. I pay attention to mood and note changes in time, content, and behavior. I aim to create vivid and realistic portraits of complex educational settings.

However, my intention is not only to inscribe a "thick description" of observed phenomena (Geertz 1973). I aim as well to convey the thoughts and feelings that I develop in the course of my observations. For example, in the excerpt below, I describe my reaction to Stephanie's introduction of a large-group reading activity in the situation that I cited earlier:

> After passing out a brief one-page story, Stephanie goes to the board and writes down different characters in the play her students are reading [*The Miracle Worker*]. After a few minutes of silent reading, and after textbooks have been distributed, Stephanie assigns different parts. "I want everybody to read today," she emphasizes as she walks back to her desk. I hear two boys in the back row respond, "I'm not reading; I don't want to read."
>
> Stephanie picks up her text and plunges ahead. "What have we learned so far in the play?" Students toss out bits and pieces of plot. "OK, why don't we continue on page 106. Do you remember what happened in the scene just before this one?" I notice that the girls in this class are responding more readily to Stephanie's promptings. Boys sit silently in the rear of the room.
>
> I make a couple of notes to myself. I observe that Stephanie stands closer to her desk than to her students. She holds onto the textbook as she asks questions about what has been covered previously. I note that Stephanie might move forward and put down her book, emphasizing to her students that she is listening to them and doing a "review" rather than "reading." I think this change might help Stephanie to get the attention of two girls on the far side of the room who talk throughout her lesson. Stephanie could walk near them and thereby signal to them that she wants everyone's attention. Dropping the textbook will position her as more of an "authority"—as a teacher who is confident in her knowledge and who gives all her attention to her students.
>
> The reading of the play begins.

Here, I focus on the suggestions that I formulated for Stephanie in response to her lesson. However, in other narratives, I question my assumptions about the nature of "good" English pedagogy, and I speculate about alternative approaches. I think mentor teachers ought to share with beginning teachers their questions and uncertainties as well as their advice. Acknowledgment of incertitude models for beginning English teachers good reflective practice, and it reminds them that pedagogical uneasiness is not always a sign of weakness or insecurity.

Do I ever inscribe summative evaluations of my beginning teachers? Yes, I do. But what I like about my storytelling approach is that summative evaluation only occurs after a sustained period of formative assessment—typically, after I have written four or five descriptive narratives. I keep my descriptive accounts in a portfolio, and I refer to them as I construct my final evaluations. With these detailed narratives in hand, I feel confident making conclusive judgments about my beginning teachers.

Do I ever discuss my evaluations with my beginning teachers? Absolutely. As good mentor teachers know, beginning English teachers like oral feedback on their teaching. I meet with my student teachers for about an hour after each observation. Often, we continue our conversations after they have had time to digest my storytelling evaluations. We refer back to the storytelling evaluations as we discuss new experiences, and sometimes I meet with small groups of student teachers in order to discuss my narratives. By the end of a semester, I have given quite a bit of critical feedback in both oral and written form.

This storytelling approach, I realize, will not suit every mentor teacher. Some teachers might find the emphasis on inquiry and collaboration too difficult or inappropriate. Others might find that they do not have enough time to write detailed descriptions of classroom practice. I believe that mentor teachers need to create their own informed approaches to the evaluation of beginning teachers.

Let me give one last indication of how I conceive this storytelling approach. In the spring of 1993, I decided to build upon the success of my initial experiments with storytelling by inviting my student teachers to write their own stories about classroom experiences. Once a week, if they desired, my student teachers could write an account of a particular English lesson. I told my student teachers to focus on description as much as possible, and I shared with them stories that I had written in previous semesters.

The response I received to this invitation was exhilarating. While some student teachers chose to write conventional journal entries, most decided to write their own storytelling evaluations. This excerpt from a story entitled "Declaration of Independence," a narrative about a class in which Valerie invited discussion about a curriculum and a series of assignments that had provoked resistance, captures the flavor of the stories I received that semester.

> "Okay, you guys . . . We need to talk. First of all, I'd like to start out by saying that you have all failed these little 'pop' quizzes . . . and the discussions from last week were not discussions at all. I simply talked to myself. So I guess what I am asking is . . . What is the problem?"
>
> The class goes into an uproar. Every student in the class is sure that he or she has the best answer to my badly phrased question.
>
> "Excuse me. Does this look like a discussion? We cannot have a discussion if everyone is talking. I am willing to discuss this, but you need to raise your hand and speak one at a time."

> The class is stunned. At first, no one says anything. The
> prospect of speaking in front of an entirely attentive class has
> succeeded in destroying each student's confidence. As usual,
> Aden comes to the rescue.

My intention in inviting this storytelling was to make the process of
critical exchange a mutual one. Student teachers, I believed, were as
capable as I was of inscribing and reflecting upon their classroom
practice. However, over the duration of the semester, I discovered that
our sharing of stories had consequences that I never anticipated. I
began to perceive my student teachers less and less as beginning
teachers, and more and more as writers with whom I shared words. In
the process, I found myself coming to a better understanding of the
problems that beginning English teachers face in their classrooms. I
listened more closely to my student teachers, and I gave them better
advice. Conversely, I began to alter my own assumptions about the
teaching of English and especially the preservice education of
prospective teachers.[2]

    Ultimately, it's this potential of stories to change the thinking of
their hearers that leads me to advocate them as a mode of evaluation.
In *Room for Maneuver: Reading (the) Oppositional (in) Narrative* (1991),
Ross Chambers proposes that storytelling can function as a means of
political agency in an alienating world (2). Chambers attributes this
potential to the fact that the desire for narration does not evaporate as
people acquire power; by telling a compelling story, he argues, story-
tellers can always subvert the thinking (and thus the actions) of more
powerful hearers (11). The potential of stories to produce social
change, Chambers proposes, far exceeds the potential of more abstract
and authoritative modes of discourse.

    As a supervisor of student teachers, I have used storytelling
techniques to persuade beginning English teachers to rethink their
pedagogy. In contrast, I myself have learned from the stories that I
have been told. Storytelling nurtures professional growth and
development, and it provides teachers with information that they
can use.

    When the 1993 spring semester came to an end, I asked my stu-
dent teachers to share with me their thoughts regarding our shared
experiment with storytelling. All of the student teachers I worked with
endorsed the idea of writing stories, while at the same time pointing
out that writing narratives as elaborate as Valerie's was time-consuming. In particular, Stephanie endorsed my storytelling approach in the
strongest possible terms:

> I definitely think that every student teacher should write stories about their experiences. Writing about what goes on in the classroom, in one's mind, or with other teachers and students is very important, not just to keep it in mind as a keepsake or memory, but to analyze, to ponder, and to question these things you write about. As future teachers, we have to reflect upon our teaching methods, our way with kids, and how we get along with other teachers or parents. *We* should continue to learn, too.

In conclusion, I would only add that the phrase "mentor teacher" might easily be substituted for "student teacher" here. As mentor teachers, we have a responsibility to make the evaluation process a learning experience—not only for our beginning teachers, but for ourselves, too. I believe that if beginning teachers are introduced to an evaluation process that encourages reflection and shared inquiry, then they will respect their work and want to continue with it. I can't think of a better method for producing reflection and shared inquiry than the activity that inspired most of us English teachers to become English teachers in the first place—reading and writing stories.

Notes

1. I hesitate to characterize my accounts of classroom observation as ethnographic narratives because of the limitations inherent in student teacher supervision. However, my storytelling approach is informed by the notion of "thick description" developed by Clifford Geertz in *The Interpretation of Cultures* (1973).

2. The most obvious assumption I altered was the notion that I should not spend too much time in my English methods class discussing classroom discipline. Without a doubt, this is the subject that student teachers most often addressed in their stories. In light of their concerns, I now give more attention to the issue of discipline.

References

Atwell, Nancie. 1987. *In the Middle: Writing, Reading, and Learning with Adolescents.* Upper Montclair, NJ: Boynton/Cook.

Chambers, Ross. 1991. *Room for Maneuver: Reading (the) Oppositional (in) Narrative.* Chicago: University of Chicago Press.

Cochran-Smith, Marilyn, and Susan L. Lytle. 1993. *Inside/Outside: Teacher Research and Knowledge.* New York: Teachers College Press.

Coles, Robert. 1989. *The Call of Stories: Teaching and the Moral Imagination.* Boston: Houghton-Mifflin.

Csikszentmihalyi, Mihalyi, Kevin Rathunde, and Samuel Whalen. 1993. *Talented Teenagers: The Roots of Success and Failure.* New York: Cambridge University Press.

Geertz, Clifford. 1973. *The Interpretation of Cultures: Selected Readings.* New York: Basic Books.

Goswami, Dixie, and Peter Stillman. 1987. *Reclaiming the Classroom: Teacher Research as an Agency for Change.* Upper Montclair, NJ: Boynton/Cook.

22 A Language for Beginning Teachers

Lisa Birnbaum
University of Tampa

With a rich array of examples, Lisa Birnbaum reflects on how she has tried to speak a language in evaluating new teachers that will not only enable a relationship of trust and confidence to grow, but will also encourage new teachers to develop their own "language for teaching."

We learn to trust our teachers through the subtle tones of support we hear in their voices and the expressions of understanding we read in their language. When I supervise beginning teachers, I want them to learn the art of building and holding trust, an art that will be needed in their work with all students, but especially those who are resistant, withdrawn, or tentative. As a teacher of writing, I approach students' work-in-progress as a respectful reader, expressing my pleasure, uncertainty, and needs. As I observe students teaching, I try to "read" their performances in the same spirit.

Responding to drafts in written commentary or one-to-one conferences has grown out of a movement to interact with student writers as they discover ideas and take risks. The work of composition theorists has taught us to listen, question, and reflect, instead of merely making judgments. Knoblauch and Brannon (1989) call this "facilitative response," in which a reader explains perceptions that a writer may consider when revising (126–130). Harris (1986) describes the teacher of writing as coach, commentator, counselor, listener, and diagnostician (35–40); and Lindemann (1982) uses the term "trusted advisor" (234). If a supervisor responds and advises in this way, a beginning teacher's class can open a process for revising performance.

My six years as a university supervisor of English interns at both a public and a private university have led me to an approach built not only upon theories of composition, but also upon qualitative research. An ethnographic researcher in the classroom, for instance, uses a technique called "participant observation," often adopting an "insider's view" (Spradley 1980, 4) of the culture participants are creating. The observer might sit with the students, adopting their perspective (as I did as a researcher and now do as a supervisor), or with the teacher, seeing and feeling from that vantage point. Other research techniques, such as triangulation—checking data with participants to ensure that perceptions are correct and to gain further insight—can help us understand, negotiate, and revise patterns of classroom communication. We ought to prepare teachers to respond to all kinds of communication in the classroom, including writing, reading, speaking aloud, and even *not* speaking. Nondirective commentary on their teaching suggests—through our language—a way to interact with their students.

I take notes during supervision, elaborate on them in a session just after the class, ask new questions, discuss concerns, make suggestions, and leave the intern with a copy of my notes. Looking back through them now, I see that there are patterns in my comments. The topics, phrases, and tones of voice illustrate a demeanor, a way of talking and writing to students that both supports and challenges them.

The voice I use is as honest as I can make it, though I am judicious, occasionally not mentioning a small problem if I want to emphasize more than one large issue (something most teachers of writing are used to doing). My voice is sympathetic, as any experienced teacher's must necessarily be. It is collegial and collaborative, a willing voice. And it is, perhaps most of all, an encouraging voice, one that understands the tremendous need of a response that says, "You're on the right track—stay on it." It is the voice of a new friend in a workplace, someone welcoming a less-experienced but able co-worker into the reality of a tough job.

At the risk of oversimplifying, I have created categories to introduce and refer to language that can be useful in broaching matters that merit response:

Suggestions

You might try . . .

Have you tried/thought of . . . ?

How about . . .?

I often like to . . .

I wonder if . . .

Consider . . .

Maybe it's a good idea to . . .

I think it's worthwhile to . . .
Might be fun to . . .
Could you have . . . ?
Will you . . . ?
Another idea is to . . .

Reflection
I'm thinking as you . . .
You seem to enjoy . . .
Students look as though . . .
I realize as I watch you that . . .
I'm curious about . . .
I sense that . . .
I see that . . .

Praise
It's good that you . . .
Great that they . . .
I like the way you . . .
You're doing very well at . . .
What an improvement since my last visit in . . .
You're doing a much better job of . . .
Creative idea to . . .
Congratulations on . . .
Impressive progress on . . .
I'm really pleased to see . . .
I enjoyed it when . . .

Criticism
Watch out for . . .
Maybe you didn't need to . . .
I don't know if I would have . . .
You may be a bit too . . .
Make sure . . .
I sense a need for/I think students need . . .
I'd like to see you do more . . .
Remember that . . .

Could you have . . . ?

Should you . . . ?

Next time, I'd try to . . .

Instead of _____, you might . . .

It's so important to/not to . . .

Keep working on . . .

_____ didn't work as well as it might have . . .

Sympathy

Too bad/How awful that . . .

I know how hard it is to . . .

I realize that . . .

I remember when I . . .

I know this is a challenge, but . . .

It's always a question for me whether to . . .

Comments may fit all five response categories, of course, and the line may blur between overlapping categories. I find that I frequently elaborate on a negative point, for instance, with questions, positive remarks, and suggestions; the most difficult of these responses (addressing unpreparedness or a lapse in judgment, for example) may be the lengthiest among my notes. Still, many of my other responses, especially suggestions, may go on at some length—often four or five sentences, sometimes cut short by a more important observation on an activity underway in the classroom. (As a classroom ethnographer for four months, I acquired skill in daily observation and descriptive note taking; for those who haven't taken notes in a busy scene, it is a quickly acquired skill.)

Another perspective—one from outside the school and without any knowledge of the students—is invaluable, even if the cooperating teacher is giving the intern detailed written and oral response each day (not common, from what my interns have reported). I act as the "insider" from outside who alternately takes the intern's side and her students' side. In the following notes to one intern, I explain what I sense as I sit with students in rows facing her (and *opposed* to her, as the first comment shows):

> They are asking good questions—be brave enough to follow through till they're satisfied.

> I get the feeling they'd like to hear each other's poems. . . . I'm dying to read some!

Praising another, I wrote:

> I'm getting the feeling I'd like to be in your class . . . you're off
> and running . . . a lot of the time I'm looking *to* you more than
> *at* you. . . . You've assumed the authority of a teacher.

> This is fun!

Below is a mixed response, from the "insider-outsider," which
includes most of the categories of commentary:

> The students appear to trust you [praise, reflection]. Try build-
> ing more rapport through personal comments [suggestion]—
> and more smiles [criticism]!

With reflective description, as free as possible of judgment, I want to
encourage evaluation of their own performances, so a part of my
response leaves space for them to start putting together what I show
them. Below I take notes as objectively as I can:

> There is talking in one part of the classroom as some write
> (some don't). Talking seems to increase. You don't address it. (Is
> journal writing a daily class opener?)

> Most work on the handout, though a couple of guys sleep. I
> wonder if you will wake them and suggest they join a group.
> Will they be able to make up the work?

For all five purposes, I try to integrate questions in commentary.
In postobservation discussion with interns, we explore their answers
and consider some of mine. This is another tool I have taken from my
work with writers in one-to-one conferences. Just as I hope student
writers will find their way without my appropriating their texts, I
want interns to make decisions about teaching that they come to after
considering my questions. The question below presents a choice:

> Have you tried ending with whole-class discussion instead of
> assigning questions to answer in writing?

Another asks for an answer that may make her aware of a need for
specific instruction:

> Have you given them guidelines for collaboration? I ask
> because they seem to be working alone and sharing occasional
> answers—not really functioning as groups.

She may tell me that she has given the class a handout on collaborative
learning, gone over it a couple of times, and despaired of finding a solution. I cannot assume that I know what I am seeing until we talk.
Working together, we can plan a strategy for the next day of group work.

Identifying with the challenges the intern faces most clearly suggests sympathy, but its fuller purpose is to open discussion about methods. When I admit to having failed at what she is attempting, I make my story of learning more compelling and my advice worth taking. Below is an example of one such comment:

> One trick I took a long time to learn was to tell them directions before grouping/pairing them. It takes careful preparation, but if you don't tell *all* of your directions to *all* of them *at once*, you'll repeat yourself throughout the hour, and some may never get the assignment straight. You'll forget something now and then, as I do, but you won't believe how much better the group work goes when you're organized and clear!

My purpose was to help her to avoid the mayhem I saw, and to show her it wasn't a failing of her students to work together or of her to design a worthwhile collaborative assignment. A small trick would do it, so I used a gentle, easygoing comment to defuse her frustration.

Gentle suggestions mask and bolster purposes that are more difficult to express to a vulnerable beginner. Below I bury disapproval of an error-ridden handout by pointing out the effect on students and avoiding direct blame:

> The typos really foul up these poor readers! Proofing was needed, though I'm sure you had too little time to retype [your cooperating teacher's] handout.

In another example, I try to inform without embarrassing:

> You may confuse them if you refer to the play as a novel.

A supervisor may be the only one to correct the intern on matters that are small but important in the impression an English teacher makes, such as regional, nonstandard expressions that she may not be aware she is using. I wrote to one intern:

> Watch nonstandard, regional speech patterns—you're using "might can" instead of "might be able to."

Critical commentary is easily softened by adding praise, such as in the following remarks:

> You introduce the piece with valuable background. Consider telling them what you like about the story, too, and why you think it's a good thing they're getting a chance to read it.

> You're explaining the text clearly, but *students* need to learn to interpret it. Let them figure out more than they think they can—you'll stretch their abilities if you let them sort out what's going on."

Since a supervisor visits several times during the semester, many comparisons can be made which help interns see change. I point out progress wherever I see it:

> Your manner seems more relaxed this visit—you know your students better, it seems.

> I'm really pleased to see that you have regained your authority in this class. The change is impressive since 3/18—in your demeanor and in theirs.

At the end of the notes, I look for ways I can sum up encouragingly. I may simply say, "You're doing *really* well," or "Good class!" though sometimes when I sense a need for more or wish to specifically applaud an intern's skill, I will extend it:

> I'm not seeing evidence of *anything* I'm concerned about. Some of what you're doing will become smoother and surer as you get experience, but I think you've got very good instincts!

> The two girls who come up to talk to you show me how well you have done in this internship. They like and trust you. Congratulations on a successful first experience in the classroom!

Becoming a teacher takes courage, and it usually shows itself in authority won before the end of the semester. Early in the experience, many interns take advantage of my open invitation to call for advice in the evening or on weekends; it is support they eventually take for granted and finally don't need. What I would hope takes its place is the desire for collaboration in future professional relationships.

The beginning of collegiality is this conversation between teachers, a conversation which deepens as we learn from each other and widens when the new teacher enters the profession. We teach the essential art of building trust with language when, as supervisors we "teach back" with expertise and sensitivity. It is through the well-chosen words of a supervisor that a beginning teacher learns a language for teaching English.

References

Harris, Muriel. 1986. *Teaching One-to-One: The Writing Conference*. Urbana, IL: National Council of Teachers of English.

Knoblauch, C. H., and Lil Brannon. 1984. *Rhetorical Traditions and the Teaching of Writing*. Upper Montclair, NJ: Boynton/Cook.

Lindemann, Erika. 1982. *A Rhetoric for Writing Teachers*. New York: Oxford University Press.

Spradley, James P. 1980. *Participation Observation*. New York: Holt, Rinehart & Winston.

23 In My Mind's Eye

Sheryl Rubin
Oceanside High School, Oceanside, New York

Sheryl Rubin looks back over nearly thirty years of dramatic and exciting changes in the way we teach and learn—changes that have freed both teachers and students, with the support of department leaders, to set out on their own odysseys of discovery.

I remember struggling as a beginning high school English teacher, in 1965, with the concept of structuring my planning to address vocabulary, grammar, literature, and composition as separate entities, assigned to different days of the week. There were, for each grade and semester, specific vocabulary lists, grammar and usage topics, and a hefty anthology; in one week, in an eleventh-grade class, I taught *Caesar and Cleopatra*, misplaced modifiers, and all the words (in alphabetical order, of course) in chapter three of *Building Word Power*. I knew then that there was something isolating in this, but I didn't know at first how to deal with it. After all, for this novice, the art of planning was a struggle in itself—each lesson in the same developmental mode: an aim, a motivation, some questions, and a summary. And I knew that when my department chair observed me, I had better follow this structure. I also knew I had to include focused questions on a literature assignment as homework. How did I know this? It was the way I had learned, and in the very same school. And so this structure kept me safe for the next few years, but it didn't stop me from thinking—Why was I asking most of the questions?

I suppose it became obvious early on to many secondary English teachers that the restrictions of traditional planning did not allow students to take responsibility for their own learning. The rumblings of the writing process were the first call to awaken teachers to the endless possibilities that control over writing brings to student reflection. A gradual restructual "revolution" is taking place in many English classrooms nationwide as students, not teachers, become the questioners, as seats are rearranged to reflect group thinking and sharing, and the strands of the integrated language arts curriculum blend in a mixture of performance, participation, and paper.

As I think about the evolution of this restructuring of the English classroom, and the impact of the integrated language arts curriculum, I recall an experience from years past that made me stray from the structure. Three years ago, well into the practice of cooperative learning and while teaching *Hamlet* to advanced placement seniors, I decided to include critical essays as a cooperative learning activity. I remembered a book of essays on the play which I had used years before in another school, with a similar class. I'll take essays from this book, I thought, assign them to groups, and spend a few days in group dialogue. When I finally located the book in my basement, I found tucked between the pages an old class list, the purple ink fading with age. On it were the names of a class from 1972, assigned to groups with instructions for a similarly structured assignment. As I placed some of the names with faces, I recalled the lively discussion they had had. And then I remembered: I had wanted my department chair to visit informally, but did not invite him because the structure of the lesson was obviously different from the norm.

I remember straying again from this norm in a team-teaching pilot with a college professor at a specialized New York City high school. In a sense, I "threw away" traditional lesson plans to wean students from a teacher-oriented classroom to a point where they were able to think critically by generating and evaluating their own ideas and to consider critically the ideas of others. Students kept journals, formulated questions, and on no occasion were provided with specific questions by the teacher. What an experience it was! We sat in a circle, listening to our students, who at one point told us they would call on us when we were needed! One student wrote, in response to an evaluation of the experience, "This class makes people think. Instead of memorizing for a test, we learn for a lifetime." Unfortunately, these ninth-grade students had to return to classes taught in the traditional, teacher-oriented mode.

Now, as chairperson of a dedicated, talented large department in a suburban high school, I get the treat of seeing the fruits of classroom restructuring—of students taking responsibility for their learning in both English and interdisciplinary classrooms. For one English/global studies tenth-grade project, students were asked to create, in groups, an ancient society. "Alive at the dawn of civilization," each group met and organized a society. Students had to include the type of religion, type of government, laws, rules, and kinds of living conditions for each society, and to show clear reasons for their need or existence. Societies included hunters and gatherers in the fertile crescent, a city-state society, and a nomadic warrior tribe. Each group prepared an oral and written project. As they continued reading about ancient civilizations in global studies, they began reading the *Odyssey* in English. In another class, students created, in groups, an odyssey that had to be set in any one of the ancient civilizations they were considering in global studies. The figurative language of these narratives was transformed into poetry and presented in class at the setting of the court of Alcinoüs.

I've seen how Whitman's use of sensory language is effective for contemporary advertising, as groups created ads using video, audiotape, choral reading, and dramatic skits; a "Meet the Press" forum, as students interviewed Emerson and Thoreau on contemporary issues; group analysis of elements of American painting in relation to character, symbol, setting, and theme in *The Crucible*; and sharing narratives based on paintings to explore the similarities between reading, writing, and the arts.

I've been treated to group creation of "Ransom Note" poems with words cut out and pasted to create image and message; to presentations of rewritten nursery rhymes using "adult" vocabulary; and to a visit to the Oprah Winfrey show to view the nature of suffering in *The Scarlet Letter*. Even Hawthorne was there to present his point of view. He wasn't there when I saw students "teach" his short stories to another class, incorporating analysis of all the elements, but he would have been pleased.

I've viewed the process of videotaping news broadcasts as a culminating assignment in a unit on nationalism in a corresponding social studies course, to hilarious presentations of Chaucer's pilgrims in the "Canterbury Feud." The Wife of Bath would have loved it! I could go on and on.

And this type of learning goes on every day in many schools nationwide. How exciting to be part of this force of expression!

I return now to the origins of my planning:

September, 1965:

> [my first novel] *Silas Marner*
> Homework Assignments: Chapters 1 and 2: How Silas' life and outlook change after he came to Raveloe? Why did he work such long hours and live in solitude?

Imagine:

September, 1993:

> *Silas Marner*
> Homework Assignments: Chapters 1 and 2: A journal entry as Silas two months after he came to Raveloe; a letter to a friend

in Lantern Yard, or to God; perhaps the creation of monologues in voices of the characters: What would Dunstan have said to defend himself? A glimpse into Eppie's diary, or Godfrey's, or a villager's inner thoughts . . . a reenactment of Silas's "trial."

What a pleasure to plan these days! The struggle is over; the structure is ours to create!

Reference

Orgel, Joseph R., and Austin M. Works. 1963. *Building Word Power.* New York: Oxford Book Company.

24 Support for New Teachers at Paul Robeson High School

Charlotte Adomaitis
Thomas Jefferson High School, Brooklyn, New York

Charlotte Adomaitis describes the support systems, including weekly "Catch Me, I'm Falling!" workshops, one-on-one mentors, and teacher publications, that have helped the faculty at an inner-city high school to stay committed and to succeed.

Support for new teachers is one of the strong attributes of the staff development program at Paul Robeson High School. This factor sets the tone for many of the innovative undertakings encouraged by the principal, Marcia Lyles.

As part of the support system for new teachers, I facilitate a weekly new teacher workshop after school, called "Catch Me, I'm Falling!" (See Appendix) I begin with a proposed topic, but after it is discussed, the new teachers digress into their classroom experiences. I use their anecdotes as problem-solving examples. Classroom-management techniques, resources in the building, and the chain of command are explained using the teachers' experiences.

These weekly opportunities for teachers to talk shop in a safe, nonjudgmental environment help to buoy them up during bad stretches and let them share their successes during good periods. These meetings lessen the isolation of the classroom and provide a more structured place than the lunchroom, where venting of unhappy experiences might take place, with little opportunity for underlying issues to be discussed.

Another new teacher program of which I am a part is mentor/intern. This differs from my group workshop because it is one-on-one. The mentoring program lasts for one semester for each pair. I am coupled with someone in my own subject area, whereas in the "Catch Me" workshop, I model answers for a variety of subject areas.

What works in both types of programs is the development of trust and having the time to hear the occurrences that new teachers needs to verbalize. It is also important that I am not a supervisor, but a high school English teacher with eighteen years of experience and a great interest in working with newcomers to the profession.

Since it helps new teachers when the school-at-large has a positive tone, I initiated a project to create a journal by teachers that would be inspirational, especially for the new teachers, who would see that teaching is an endless progression of individual influences. I sent out a call to our faculty for articles describing the teacher who most influenced them and the qualities which that teacher embodied that they could see reflected in their own teaching. Easily half our faculty contributed. The resulting journal is called "I Remember a Teacher. . . ."

Great beginnings for new teachers exist in a positive environment where there are periods for extended communication. Questions like "How are you doing?" and "What's on your mind today?" work wonders when teachers set aside their paperwork to listen for an hour or two to someone describing something good about their chosen profession or discussing how to handle a problem.

Many teachers come to Paul Robeson with no intention of staying because of the difficult inner-city conditions of the Bedford-Stuyvesant/Crown Heights area. However, the support system of the administration is so nurturing that very few leave.

It is teachers coaching teachers that makes our "great beginnings" work.

APPENDIX

Catch Me! I'm Falling
New Teacher Workshop

Session 1: Overview and Introduction
Inventory of problems encountered by new teachers
Date: September 28, 1993

Session 2: Human Relations—Protocol for Success (especially with APs, parents, support staff, etc.)
Date: October 5, 1993

Session 3: Classroom Management, Lesson Plans, Grades
Date: October 12, 1993

Session 4: The Guidance Department—How It Can Help the New Teacher
(Guest Speaker: Guidance Counselor)
Date: October 19, 1993

Session 5: The UFT—How The Union Helps the New Teacher
(Guest Speaker: Mr. Hinds, UFT Chapter Chair)
Date: October 26, 1993

Session 6: Peer Mediation for Students: How It Works
(Guest speaker)
Date: November 2, 1993

Session 7: SPARK
(Guest Speaker: Jackie Williams, SPARK Coordinator)
Date: November 9, 1993

Session 8: Business House—What is it? How Knowledge of the Liaisons That
Paul Robeson High School Has Created Helps the Vision of the New Teacher
(Guest speaker: Ms. Leonard, AP Supervisor-Business)
Date: November 16, 1993

Session 9: What Do You Do if a Student . . . ?
Date: November 23, 1993

Session 10: Technology House–What Is It? How Knowledge of the Liaisons
That Paul Robeson High School Has Created Helps the Vision of the New
Teacher (Guest Speaker: Dr. Isom, AP Supervisor-Technology)
Date: November 30, 1993

Session 11: The Dean's Office—How the New Teacher Can Use the Discipline
Sector of the School (Guest speaker: Mr. Kazlowski, Dean)
Date: December 7, 1993

Session 12: Mastery of the Lesson Plan
Date: December 14, 1993

Session 13: Portfolio Assessment
(Guest Speaker: Roberta Koza, AP Supervisor-English)
Date: December 21, 1993

Session 14: Meaningful Grades
(Guest Speaker: Dr. Lyles, Principal)
Date: January 4, 1994

Session 15: The Duties of the Exam Proctor; Special School Schedules;
Marking Committees
Date: January 11, 1994

Session 16: The New Term—A Chance to Start Over
Date: February 1, 1994

Session 17: Homerooms: How to Set the Tone for the Entire School
Date: February 8, 1994

Session 18: The Library
(Guest Speaker: Dr. Knight, Librarian)
Date: February 15, 1994

Session 19: Teacher Expectations: How Do You Convey Your Expectations to
Your Students?
(Guest Speaker: Lisa Gibbs, Second-Year Teacher)
Date: March 1, 1994

Session 20: Criteria for High School Diplomas
(Guest Speaker: Ms. Taylor, Guidance Counselor)

Date: March 8, 1994

Session 21: Questioning Techniques
(Guest Speaker: Derissa Davis)
Date: March 15, 1994

Session 22: Different Learning Styles—How This Impacts on Behavior Management
(Guest Speaker: Rosemarie Curley, Congruence Specialist)
Date: March 22, 1994

Session 23: Alternative Teaching Strategies
Date: March 29, 1994

Session 24: The Observation—Your Official Evaluation
Date: April 12, 1994

Session 25: Your Personal Professional Goals in the Teaching Profession
Date: April 19, 1994

Session 26: Self-Evaluation—How Far Have You Progressed as a Teacher Since September?
(Teachers will write answers to an evaluation instrument)
Date: April 26, 1994

25 Beginning Teacher Support Programs: Bridging Preservice and Inservice

Susan A. Wasserman
California State University—Northridge

Susan Wasserman, recognizing the enormous stress placed on beginning teachers, identifies some of the features of a California State University program designed to bridge their preservice and inservice experiences and provide support when they most need it.

Demands placed upon beginning teachers are so insurmountable that 35–50 percent of new teachers "drop out" of the profession in their first five to seven years. This should not come as a surprise. It is actually understandable. One day the teacher is a student in a carefully guided university teacher preparation program—a few days later, the first-year teacher must assume the same duties and responsibilities of a twenty- to thirty-year veteran teacher.

Does this mean that colleges and universities have failed to prepare their students—prospective teachers—adequately for the realities of the classroom? This was definitely the theory held by school districts, state departments of education or education agencies, legislators at state and national levels, and lay people alike. During the past few years, however, this view has begun to change, and there is a realization that novice teachers cannot necessarily be prepared to step into the classrooms of our complex schools and function any more effectively than they actually do—another important element must be added to their preparation. What is that needed element which will help ensure teacher effectiveness, high morale, and positive job satisfaction? The needed element may very well be a support component, a bridge between preservice and inservice, which is essential to the continued professional development of beginning teachers. Perhaps, it also may be the key to stemming the tide of those leaving the profession.

Bridging Preservice and Inservice

"On the opening day of school, they changed my room, grade level, and group of children. The support person you sent to help me is a 'saint'—without her, I wouldn't have been able to survive!" So wrote a beginning teacher to the director of a university new teacher project. Another new teacher reported, "I never thought anyone at the university would contact me *after* I started teaching. I not only received a call—but my university student teaching supervisor is visiting me and helping me. It's nice to know there are people who care."

Many such comments are received by California State University–Northridge concerning the support provided to new teachers through CSUN teacher support projects. These are just two of such comments indicating the tremendous need for programs which create a bridge between preservice education and inservice experience during the first, second, and third years of teaching. New teachers *need* and *want* this support. This support should be made available to every beginning teacher nationwide.

Types of Teacher Support Programs

Only eight to ten years ago, such programs either did not exist or were few in number. Fortunately, today, there are a great many new teacher support programs operating nationwide. They vary in terms of funding sources; sponsoring agencies; organizational patterns; support components provided; role, status, and function of persons as support providers; length of time support continues; and the manner in which support, assessment, and evaluation are separated or linked. These are but a few factors which mark differences in support programs. Should support programs be more uniform? Certainly, we can learn much from the variety of programs which have been developed by colleges and universities, school districts, teachers' unions, community groups, and various partnerships made up of these diverse groups. Successful programs/projects have certain components in common, but there are definitely distinctive features which are tailored specifically to the particular context of the districts, schools, and classrooms. This is a strength rather than a weakness—a program which can be developed to meet specific needs. However, there are many features of support programs which are transferable—and easily adapted/adopted.

Description of CSUN Support Programs

The School of Education, California State University–Northridge, has a number of support programs, only four of which will be briefly described here. The first, the *Beginning Teacher Support Program: Help-Line*, was initiated in 1985. This program can be utilized by any teacher: a graduate of the CSUN Teacher Preparation program, a graduate of any other college or university program, an emergency credential teacher, a beginning or any other teacher experiencing problems, or any teacher just desiring support. The program has grown from supporting thirty teachers in its first year to supporting 125 to 135 teachers on an ongoing basis at the school site in recent years. It also provides monthly workshops with 200 to 400 in attendance and a monthly newsletter received by over 4,000 new teachers, veteran teachers, and student teachers.

The *California New Teacher Project* was developed in 1990 as a partnership between CSUN, Los Angeles Unified School District (LAUSD), and the union United Teachers, Los Angeles (UTLA). This program was funded by the California Department of Education and the Commission on Teacher Credentialing. It provided supportive services to thirty-five teachers each year, all selected graduates of CSUN. There were thirty-seven such projects throughout California.

The *Beginning Teacher Support and Assessment Program* was initiated in 1993. It also is a three-way partnership between CSUN, LAUSD and UTLA and is funded by the state. It supports fifty first- and second-year teachers annually. These teachers are graduates of CSUN and other universities, as well as emergency credential teachers, most of whom teach in bilingual classrooms. This program has an assessment component, as mandated by the state, in addition to the support component.

Many of the support components of the above three projects are listed in another section of this essay.

The *Comprehensive Teacher Institute*, initiated in 1989, is a tripartite collaboration between the CSUN School of Education, the CSUN academic departments, and LAUSD. This program differs most from the other support programs in that students, prospective teachers who are juniors and seniors, are mentored during their undergraduate programs: liberal studies or specific content areas. Next, they are mentored through their postbaccalaureate work, student teaching and intern program. In their first year(s) of teaching with a preliminary or clear credential, they are provided continued support in their classrooms.

Components of Support Programs

There are a number of components which are an integral part of the CSUN Beginning Teacher programs, but not all are included in all of the programs. Following are some of the components characteristic of one or more of the programs:

- University supervisors, whose former students are in the project, visit the new teachers and work with them during the school year. Already having a positive relationship with their former student(s), professors are able to provide positive feedback as well as suggestions to the new teachers concerning effective teaching practices. In this way, new teachers are more apt to utilize effective techniques and strategies they learned in university coursework and student teaching. Whenever certain problems confront the new teachers, they can call and seek specific suggestions. Because there is no evaluation made by the university supervisor, most new teachers welcome and implement such suggestions. (This particular feature is usually not provided to emergency credentialed teachers as they have not completed a regular teacher preparation program and might not be able to benefit as greatly from such assistance.)

    One university professor stated, "It's so nice to be able to get out and see former university students during their first year of teaching. It helps us know that what we are teaching is effective. We can also make certain changes in our coursework. It gives us the opportunity to continue to be of help to former students whose success is so important to us here at the university." This outreach of the preservice program serves to help new teachers utilize in the "real world" the successful methodologies, strategies, and techniques learned in university methods courses and student teaching.

- Another unique feature of these projects is the utilization of retired teachers to visit and work with new teachers in their classrooms on an ongoing basis. (All four of the support programs discussed have this component.) A close professional relationship quickly develops between the "seasoned" teachers and the beginning teachers. There is a bond of trust which soon grows. The "saint" mentioned previously by one of the new teachers is a member of this Cadre of Retired

Educators (CORE). When possible, the retired teacher begins her or his supportive work prior to or on the opening days of school. In this way, help can be focused on everything from bulletin boards, room arrangement, learning centers, organization, scheduling, short- and long-range planning, and ideas and materials for working effectively with children of diverse backgrounds and other languages.

The retired teacher is *always* there for the new teacher—either by phone or in person. When asked why she has become a member of CORE, this "helping" group member stated, "I want to repay in some small way some of the people who helped me." Another retired teacher declared, "I wish I had been given this type of help. It was sink or swim when I began teaching." "You know, it's harder to teach today than it was when I began teaching," lamented another retired educator. "So much is expected of these young people. I'm glad to be able to help."

- On-site teachers ("buddies") are rewarded for their help to new teachers with recognition and a stipend. One such teaching colleague stated, "I've been helping new teachers at my school for years. I have never before been 'recognized' for this. What a nice thing to do. Thank you." These on-site colleagues are a tremendous help in assisting new teachers to become accepted members of the faculty; in addition, "buddies" help their new colleagues in the solution of daily school-related problems.

- Administrative support of new teachers is enhanced because these programs are a partnership between their school district and the university. As such district and region representatives lend their support to this joint effort. They work closely with their site administrators, whose schools are involved, to provide as much administrative support for each of the new teachers as possible.

- "Released days" are provided for new teachers. Four to six of these days, depending upon the budget, include classroom observations of experienced teachers coupled with inservice sessions on specific topics, i.e., "Thematic Instruction," "Integrating Math and Science," "Writing Process and Writers' Workshop," "Bilingual Education," and "ESL and Sheltered English." Classroom management is emphasized at each of these released days.

- Funds are provided for educational materials purchased by the new teachers for use in their classrooms. This is particularly appreciated by the new teachers as they can secure materials that are not necessarily available to them through the district.

■ A one-unit university credit can be earned for attendance at five workshops held at CSUN for new teachers. The teachers learn much at these workshops; as well, such units can be accumulated and utilized toward pay increments as new teachers climb the career ladder.

■ A portion of the registration fee for attendance at conferences sponsored by local, state, or national teacher organizations is reimbursed to new teachers to encourage participation in professional activities. In addition, a portion of the fee for membership in a teacher organization is also returned to the new teacher. In this manner, it is hoped that new teachers will begin early in their careers to feel a part of the teaching profession.

Types of Problems/Challenges

Among the many challenges and problems faced by new teachers, the following appear to be experienced by a vast number of such teachers:

Meeting the Needs of Individual Children

Tremendous diversity exists in classrooms today. Children in many schools, especially urban schools, have different experiential, language, and cultural backgrounds. Although this diversity can be utilized as a strength in any school program, it can also be a daily challenge in meeting the specific needs of each child.

Children also vary greatly in scholastic ability and achievement, attention span and ability to "stay on task." There are also many children in any classroom who may evidence certain learning disabilities. These and many other factors make it extremely difficult for teachers who want sincerely to meet the needs of every child in the classroom, thus assuring success for each student.

Problems in Classroom Management

Every teacher must be well versed in a variety of classroom-management strategies and techniques. Children often "try out" a beginning teacher just because she or he is new to a school and has not established a reputation and relationships with children and their parents. This can be very stressful for the beginning teacher who wants to be "liked" by the children, yet who realizes the importance of having a classroom climate in which she or he can teach and the children can learn.

Therefore, the teacher often must utilize an inordinate amount of time establishing and maintaining classroom control in the large-group setting (often thirty to forty children), thus allowing for teaching/learning to be facilitated in the total group small group and/or with individual children.

Teachers must work constructively with individual children who evidence overt deviant behaviors, while not detracting from the total group. This may include working with children who have severe emotional and/or physical problems. Some of these children may indeed be at risk: children who were "drug babies," students involved in gang activities, and those who are engaged in drug and alcohol abuse.

Classroom management is more than control and discipline alone. Problems often arise for the new teacher because of lack of supplies, books, and equipment and even furniture not being available in the first days of school.

Extremely Demanding Assignments

Often new teachers are given assignments which would be demanding even for a veteran teacher. It is said that a new teacher usually gets the children assigned to her or him that other teachers prefer not to have. New teachers are also assigned to combination grades/split grades, where two or more grade levels are grouped to make one class. Classes designated as "bilingual" or "modified bilingual" are given to the new teacher even if that teacher is monolingual. (A class may have as many as seventeen or more language groups represented.)

Even more distressing, after the new teacher has taught her class successfully for several weeks or months, school reorganization occurs, and the teacher loses her class of children, and the process of establishing good classroom management begins anew. The grade level(s) even may be changed—not once, but perhaps several times during the school year. Often, new teachers have a change of grade levels at the beginning of each year as well, even though veteran teachers might teach the same grade for years. Beginning teachers can also be "bumped" to other schools anytime during their first year(s) of teaching.

Not mentioned previously is the fact that new teachers are often "rovers" for an entire year. This means that the teacher moves from classroom to classroom many times during the year-round school calendar, thus not having her or his own classroom to call "home."

Overload of Paperwork

Almost all new teachers cite an endless stream of paperwork as an acute problem. This includes, but is not limited to, maintaining the school classroom register, attendance cards, cumulative records, grade rosters, individual or class profiles, correcting papers, preparing files of children's work for each content area to show parents at Back-to-School Night, an open house, and parent conferences, as well as the tedious preparation of report cards. This does not even include the abundance of records for special local, state, and federal programs in which the school may be involved.

Lack of Time

New teachers, when asked what they need most, usually answer, "More time!" They point out that there just isn't time enough in each day, week, month, semester, or school year to teach all of the areas of the curriculum as designated by state frameworks and district curriculum guides. Beginning teachers also feel they need time for extracurricular demands such as faculty meetings, department and grade-level meetings, ongoing conferencing with parents of children experiencing problems, involvement in after-school events such as PTA meetings, school fund-raisers, and other school and community activities.

Further, additional time is needed to attend university classes, district inservice sessions, and conferences and workshops in order to continue the professional growth so needed to be on the cutting edge of educational practice.

Lack of Administrative Support

Due to an extremely busy schedule, the site administrator seems, at times, unable to give the needed support that all new teachers require. In actuality, many administrators, although they would like to personally provide support to the new teachers in his or her school, are able to do little more than be pleasant and advise the teacher of the dates that she or he will be visited for evaluation! Many of the occurrences cited under the other problems might be alleviated if the principal, the school management team, and other willing teachers, parents, and staff worked together to accomplish some of the following:

- New teachers could be assigned an on-site, helpful ("buddy") teaching colleague.
- New teachers would not be assigned as "rovers" during their first years.

- Willing veteran teachers would be given the more challenging grade levels, and the cluster of children needing a great deal of added attention would be divided among experienced teachers rather than having children with overt behavior problems assigned to the new teacher.

- Time, effort, and any money available would be utilized to obtain the necessary materials and equipment to prepare a new teacher's classroom.

- Creative planning by the principal could make time available to the new teacher for planning, preparation of materials, attendance at district meetings and inservices, and observations of proven, effective teachers at the new teacher's own school as well as other schools.

- The principal could refrain from expecting new teachers to assume committee posts or other activities which necessitate much added time.

- The new teacher could be assigned the same grade level, if the teacher is comfortable and successful in that grade, for at least a few years, whenever possible.

- An orientation to the school and all needed paperwork and documents would be given at the beginning of the school year and during the school year, as other files, records, and the like are required, i.e., reports cards, cumulative card entries, etc.

Success for New Teachers

There is little wonder why new teachers become stressed out during those crucial first years of teaching. In a list of the ten top stressful occupations, being a high school teacher was number one! Certainly, it is evident that all teachers at any grade level are under stress and that beginning teachers experience high levels of stress.

"I keep reading and being told that we need to be reflective teachers. I believe in that—but I wish I knew how to find the time to be reflective," so stated a new teacher at the end of her first few months of teaching. She then paraphrased Scarlet O'Hara, in *Gone with the Wind*, by saying, "I'll think about that—tomorrow. Now, I just want to find ways to survive—and *time* to think!"

Support programs which bridge preservice educational coursework and student teaching with the inservice (first years in the classroom) will ease the induction period for beginning teachers. (These programs, when tailored for the emergency credential teachers, are exceedingly important.) By helping new teachers toward greater teaching effectiveness and by helping them maintain a positive attitude toward their chosen profession, it can be expected that students will be more apt to achieve to their fullest ability and establish and maintain a lifelong love of learning and a valuing of the school experience. The education profession may even be the more attractive profession it should be. Then the best candidates will be attracted to teaching, and the best teachers will remain in the profession.

References

Gold, M. J., and B. Pepin. 1987. *Passing the Torch: Retired Teachers as Mentors for New Teachers.* New York: Center for Advanced Study in Education, City University of New York.

Morey, Ann, and Diane Murphy, eds. 1990. *Designing Programs for New Teachers: The California Experience.* San Francisco: Far West Laboratory for Educational Research and Development.

Schlechty, P., and V. Vance. 1983. "Recruitment, Selection and Retention: The Shape of the Teaching Force." *Elementary School Journal* 83: 469–87.

Veenman, S. 1984. "Perceived Problems of Beginning Teachers." *Review of Educational Research* 54: 143–78.

Wasserman, Susan A., and Donna W. Emery. 1992. "Help-Line: A University-Based Beginning Teacher Support Program." *Teacher Education Quarterly* 19.

26 Just Ten Minutes a Day (On Becoming a Teacher/Writer)

Noreen Duffy Copeland
Holy Ghost Catholic School, Albuquerque, New Mexico

Noreen Duffy Copeland's study group learned how valuable writing their "first-year teacher stories" could be not only to themselves and to the teachers who would come after them, but also to the students whose teachers had gained new respect for the difficult process of becoming writers.

How do you ever find the time to write? I never have time to do anything else that isn't connected to teaching."

The overburdened voices of the eight novice teachers haunted me as I attempted to lead them down the path to becoming teacher/writers. As part of a study group which they attended in order to complete a master's degree in elementary education from the University of New Mexico, they were being asked to write a "First-Year Teacher Story" which would become a legacy for the next group of beginning teachers, a kind of sneak preview of coming attractions. At the same time, I hoped that this firsthand experience of the writing process would affect the way they viewed the writing process for their own students.

The teachers in the study group had been meeting twice a month since August, sharing their concerns and successes and also discussing a variety of topics: discipline, classroom management, assessment and evaluation, conferencing with parents, communications with colleagues, etc. During February's study group I gave each teacher a new thirty-nine cent spiral notebook, hoping to provide a special place for them to record their reflections of their daily classroom experiences—in Lucy McCormick Calkins's words, giving the teachers "a concrete physical invitation to write" (Calkins and Harwayne 1991, 38). There was much negotiation over the particular colors: "I'll take the blue one." "I'd like the green one." "Are you going to keep that turquoise one you're holding in your hand for yourself, because I'd like that color?" Janet summarized the others' enthusiasm when she stated, "No one has ever given me a special notebook just for myself."

I then introduced a prewriting activity which I had learned from another teacher who, like me, was a participant in the 1992–93 Rio Grande Writing Project at the University of New Mexico. I asked the novice teachers to recall some of the memorable moments in their classrooms since the beginning of the year and to begin writing about their remembrances. After writing for about five minutes, I asked the teachers to stop and read what they had written and choose a phrase, an idea, or a sentence and begin writing again, focusing in greater detail on the self-selected thought. For approximately thirty minutes the teachers continued this process of writing, reading, focusing on a new idea and writing about it.

Like all teacher/writers wishing to follow the writing process, I knew the next step was to introduce sharing. I first read a poem that I had been working on and asked for comments from the group. After providing this modeling, I invited each teacher who was comfortable with sharing some of his or her writing to read a selection to the group. Carolyn prefaced her piece with "I'll read mine, but you've got to promise you won't laugh." "This may sound a little crazy but . . . here goes," and Percilla began a description of her students' confused faces as they entered the classroom after she had changed the entire environment for the fifth time within a month. Thus began the first agonizing steps of teacher/writers taking a risk to share their pieces with one another.

Before leaving for the evening I encouraged the novice teachers to write for ten minutes each day, reflecting on the day's events. I acknowledged that I was familiar with the difficulty of this assignment because I constantly struggled to make time for my own daily writing as I, too, tried to develop within myself the habits of a teacher/writer.

During study group over the following months the teachers read their drafts, learned from other prewriting activities, received feedback from their colleagues, abandoned pieces, rewrote, edited, revised because of others' suggestions, etc.

Almost three months later the first-year teacher stories were ready for publication. Lori described her first field trip with her fifth graders to the state capital, where the tour guides exhibited looks of surprise when she introduced herself as the person in charge. Shawnda captured the growth of a student who receives special education speech and language services from "shy one," to volunteering to help the storyteller at the public library before an audience of fifty. Jami recalled the teachers who touched her own life and described her hopes for what she wishes her students to always remember and carry with them from Ms. Jacobson's second-grade class. Everyone could empathize with Janet, who compared her first year teaching to a roller coaster ride. Carolyn composed an open letter to her students. Pablo's story recaptured his own first-grade experience in Ecuador and compared it with the feelings of his students as they entered a newly reopened school building, holding tightly to their parents' hands. The poem about Percilla's student, emotionally hurting Delilah, touched a nerve in each of us as we identified our own Deliliahs. "Metamorphosis," Kelly's contribution, was a testimony to the necessity of teachers providing a nurturing environment for all students, especially the fragile ones. With words, each teacher had created a glimpse of his or her first experiences entering into the world of children and teaching and writing.

In order to determine how their own experience of writing the first-year teacher story may have affected the novice teachers' views of the writing process and its application to the classroom, I conducted brief interviews, asking teachers to share what they had learned.

All of the teachers mentioned the importance of the level of trust which had been established within the study group. A teacher described her past anxiety over someone rejecting her personal stories as an adolescent. She talked about the importance of controlling what she could say and share and, especially, *not* share with the group. Another testified to the comfortable familiarity within the group because

> We had discussed strengths and weaknesses, concerns and needs throughout the year. It was easier to share. No one was going to pull out their red pen and make your paper bleed.

Another teacher believed that the writing process helped to build friendships, that they had gotten to know each other on a different level.

The notebook was useful to several of the teachers as an organizational tool and an idea book:

> The notebook helped me to be more organized. I knew everything was going to be in that notebook. When I abandoned my poem I kept coming back to what I had written about Thomas. Those lines and sentences and new material made up my story.

Carolyn stated, "I wouldn't know where I would have started. It was almost like keeping a journal of my experiences and feelings." Pablo described the notebook as his writing diary, full of different ideas. The notebooks helped teachers to develop a consciousness about their teaching and its impact on their own lives that Lucy McCormick Calkins describes in *Living between the Lines*:

> My life belongs to me, it matters. I need to put scraps of time and thought away in order to take them out later, to live with and linger with them. (36–37)

Several teachers discovered the value of establishing a consistent time and location for their daily writing and consequently for their students' writing. The recliner in the den, the dining-room table, and in bed just before surrendering to exhaustion became the physical spaces that set the writers to task. Shawnda, a second-grade teacher, said,

> It helped me to sit in the same place every day because it determined the activity. I learned that consistency is important, and now in the classroom, we pass the journals out and the kids go to their desks or to the same spot in the room. I used to *just fit* writing in at different times during the day. Now we do it at the same time.

Carolyn also noticed that the environment made a difference in her own writing and related this to her own classroom practice: "The students, too, need to go where they're comfortable before they start to write.

Sharing their writings with their peers in study group also had an impact on students' sharing writing in the classroom: "I learned that not sharing was okay. I know that given time, the students will share." "Now I try to spotlight their writing and give them a chance to share. Before, we used to share just once in a while."

In addition to sharing becoming a more routine part of their students' writing process, teachers began to emulate the same kind of responses toward their students' pieces that they had practiced when responding to other novice teachers during the study group. Lori said, "I've really been trying to point out positives to the kids, even when I talk about mechanics." Kelly, a kindergarten teacher, said that the response part was important to her personally:

> It gave me encouragement when I could try things out on an audience. The audience hears parts that I may not hear, or the audience may suggest other ideas. The response part helped me to focus my kids on being a positive audience.

Carolyn summarized her thoughts about sharing:

> Hearing someone else express an opinion about my writing put me in the seat of being a student and understanding what I'm asking them to do. It's important to respect the writer and the piece.

Reading their pieces aloud as they shared their notebooks and drafts became a strategy that several of the teachers practiced with their own students:

> Reading out loud became really important for my students. When you read silently, you can miss when the rhythm of the piece is broken or there are obvious mistakes, like missing words. Now I invite my children to go out to the patio to read it out loud. They're able to self-correct and come back to me and say "Oh yeah, *huh*, Ms. Dalsaso."

A fifth-grade teacher also noticed that insisting that the children read their writings aloud to her helped with whole pages of run-on sentences, punctuation, and verb agreement: "I'd say to them, 'Wait, you stopped and took a breath, but there's no period there.' "

During our final study group, as I looked around the table at the proud faces of the novice teachers handing in their finished pieces, wanting to share just one more draft and reflecting on what they learned about themselves, their students, and the writing process, I knew that their stories would indeed be a legacy for the next generation of first-year teachers. More important, I knew that their own writing experiences had affected the implementation of the writing process in their classrooms. As they grew more comfortable in their roles as teacher/writers, they began to understand what they were requesting of their own students as they lead them down the path to becoming student/writers.

Reference

Calkins, Lucy McCormick, with Shelley Harwayne. 1991. *Living between the Lines*. Portsmouth, NH: Heinemann.

27 Using the Teaching Portfolio to Enhance the Development of Student Teachers

John Zubizarreta
Columbia College

John Zubizarreta argues for the value of the teaching portfolio as a method by which both novice and experienced teachers can reflect upon and document their philosophies, their goals, their successful and also less-than-successful efforts, and their growth as teachers.

Young teachers should know that teaching portfolios are an effective tool for simultaneously improving instruction in novice as well as seasoned teachers and providing a supportive, convincing method of evaluation. The dramatic increase in institutions using portfolios for improvement and assessment of teaching demonstrates that such documents ably serve the needs of both instructors seeking ways of documenting teaching effort to help them develop in the profession and administrators who need more reliable evaluation of teaching performance. In his recent book *Successful Use of Teaching Portfolios,* Peter Seldin (1993) notes that in contrast to the "75 institutions thought to be using portfolios just two years ago," as many as "400 colleges and universities . . . are now using or experimenting with portfolios" (4). Many recognized American scholars such as Ernest Boyer, Lynne Cheney, Peter Seldin, and key figures of the American Association for Higher Education have touted the benefits of teaching portfolios in helping to shape exemplary teaching careers and define viable criteria for evaluation of instruction. Canadian educators have known the practical rewards of teaching dossiers for two decades, and Dalhousie University's comprehensive use of dossiers for faculty development and personnel decisions is a model program illustrating the impact of portfolios on both beginning and experienced teaching careers.

Many veteran faculty have written portfolios for practical improvement; for revaluation of specific methods and outcomes in designated courses; for documentation of teaching in yearly reviews; for reflection about pedagogical or methodological experiments; or (as in the real case of one distinguished, retired teacher in a North Carolina school) for the sake of leaving a legacy of valuable experience to junior faculty who need direction in learning what does or does not work in certain courses, what teaching enhancement opportunities exist in a department, and what aspects of the job are worth careful study to help a young teacher adjust and grow effectively. But the beginning teacher certainly stands to gain even more from a teaching portfolio in that it serves as a catalyst for substantive improvement in teaching philosophy, methods, and goals. Also, the ability of the portfolio to provide outside readers with concise, selective, evidence-based information from a wide variety of sources gives the novice instructor a highly individualized, credible, and factual document for the purpose of evaluation.

The Contents of a Beginner's Portfolio

The portfolio is an evidence-based narrative document in which a faculty member concisely organizes details of teaching accomplishment and effort. Most effective portfolios are about eight double-spaced pages that offer selected information about a teacher's assigned responsibilities; philosophy; methods; materials; student products that empirically demonstrate learning; evaluations from students, peers, and supervisors; special development efforts, professional workshops, and classroom experiments; and realistic teaching goals. Selective information does not mean culled, biased details but rather fair and generous representation. Even the occasional flop is worthy material for a formative portfolio, especially if the portfolio-as-process reveals genuine adjustment and growth, if the teacher has articulated innovation and risk as key components of a teaching philosophy, and if the school recognizes experimentation and change as signals of vitality in good teaching. In any case, an appendix contains all the hard-copy information that concretely supports the narrative and balances claims with evidence. Since each portfolio invites cogent reflection about individual teaching values and tactics, each document bears signature items that personalize the document and provide a unique profile of each teacher. Consequently, every portfolio is as different as every teacher. A representative table of contents (see Figure 1) for both a beginner and expert may include the following headings:

Teaching Portfolio

Name
Department
School
Date

Table of Contents

1. Assigned Teaching Responsibilities
2. Reflective Statement of Teaching Philosophy
3. Methods and Strategies
4. Description of Course Materials: Syllabuses, Assignments, Handouts
5. Products: Evidence of Student Learning
6. Student and Peer Evaluations
7. Professional Development of Teaching: Conferences, Workshops, Revisions, and Experiments
8. Short- and Long-Term Teaching Goals
9. Appendices

Figure 1. Sample table of contents for portfolio.

Of course, the items selected shift in importance, content, and development, according to the instructor's depth of experience and purpose for writing a portfolio. Beginning teachers can use the portfolio advantageously because it is a living document that charts an instructor's developing responsibilities and other dimensions of teaching. As new items are added, old ones are removed; as old goals are achieved, new ones are added. The portfolio becomes a process of constant reflection and specifically documented action concerning one's teaching. For more ideas about what to include in a portfolio, one may consult Seldin's most recent book or his earlier *The Teaching Portfolio: A Practical Guide to Improved Performance and Promotion/Tenure Decisions* (1991); the AAHE's *The Teaching Portfolio: Capturing the Scholarship in Teaching* (1991); the Canadian Association of University Teachers' *The Teaching Dossier: A Guide to Its Preparation and Use* (1986); Carol O'Neil and Alan Wright's *Recording Teaching Accomplishment: A Dalhousie Guide to the Teaching Dossier* (1991); or Floyd Urbach's "Developing a Teaching Portfolio" (1992), all of which can be adapted to meet the special needs of trainees or working beginners in K–12.

Beginning a Portfolio

Regardless of the purposes or signature items that personalize each portfolio according to varied teaching values, styles, and academic disciplines, the narrative body of the portfolio provides all teachers an opportunity for reflection about *what* and *how* they teach, but more important, *why*, an essential critical process culminating in an act of writing that has its own intrinsic worth in enhancing the quality of both novice and expert teaching. The portfolio also includes a valuable appendix of documentation that supports the narrative. Both the narrative and appendix, however, consist of selective information and data; as new items are added, old ones are removed, keeping the portfolio current, which is why a date in the heading is important, establishing a reference point against which to evaluate information about responsibilities, awards, classroom accomplishments, student ratings, development efforts, or goals.

A single container is strongly recommended—an ample three-ring binder or an accordion legal folder is an excellent cover that provides security and flexibility, encouraging concise management of materials in separately labeled sections with identification tabs for the narrative and appendices. If a portfolio requires additional space for supplemental materials such as audio- or videotapes, then the instructor may briefly discuss such items in the narrative and refer readers to a designated location in a departmental file or supervisor's office for additional materials. Having the narrative portion of the portfolio on computer disk is handy because if a teacher needs part of the portfolio— for example, a statement of philosophy for a teaching award, a description of methods and goals for a grant or fellowship, or a supervisor's request for a beginning teacher to submit periodic analyses of class evaluations—then the appropriate section is easily printed from the disk.

Before compiling information for a coherent, credible portfolio, the novice teacher begins the process of written reflection (the initial and most important step in developing a portfolio) and recognizes that a sound portfolio balances (1) materials from self, (2) materials from others, and (3) products of student learning. Materials from self come easily because the teacher controls information such as statements of responsibilities, philosophy, and methods. Materials from others are mostly out of the individual's control, since they are comprised of student and peer or administrative ratings and comments. In gathering such materials, the new teacher should consider building a track record of formative evaluations from peers both inside and outside the home department; from individuals in other schools or in the community, observers who can comment on teaching-related performance; from alumni or alumnae knowledgeable about one's instruction; and from supervisors who should carefully and supportively write detailed, periodic analyses of junior teachers after regular, candid meetings designed to promote improvement.

The most difficult area to address is the products of student learning, which is why authentic, rigorous assessment is so confounding to the beginning teacher. Often dizzied by the daunting pace of a new professional academic life, most beginners do not think about the importance of analyzing student products from a baseline to determine actual growth. However, products of learning—that is, hard evidence of the impact of teaching intervention in students' work and progress—is a vital component in a portfolio that attempts to define both the wide scope of accomplishment and the unique qualities of a particular teacher.

Young teachers wonder how they can develop a worthwhile portfolio without extensive experience. But the truth is that teachers training for elementary or secondary school jobs and graduate assistants preparing for postsecondary positions can write remarkably convincing and detailed portfolios that include plenty of substantive information as well as reasonable teaching goals. Even without experience in a secured job, a serious student teacher has had enough courses, has observed enough varied instructional strategies, and has thought enough about teaching to write a viable philosophy in which the beginner can articulate contemplated values. In apprenticeship years, beginners try different techniques in their classes, picking and choosing among the various strategies of their peers and mentors, grounding them in a number of methodologies that form the basis for reflection and projected action in a portfolio's section on methods. Beginners also have syllabuses, assignment sheets, and handouts used in their first classes, materials that—no matter how raw or how few at first—help the instructor reflect upon the pedagogical motive and effectiveness of daily classroom work. Additionally, the undergraduate trainee in a practicum setting has access to course and instructor evaluations written, if not by students, then by the supervising lead teacher. Such rating forms facilitate improvement, and concise analysis of evaluations in a portfolio is a key step in becoming a self-conscious, careful teacher. If young teachers quickly learn the rationale and value of portfolios in a supportive setting, they will also figure out the importance of student products in charting improvement and in providing valid assessment. Such insight may prompt the beginning teacher to be a more thorough, detailed observer of student learning, a more deliberate and formative grader of student work, and a more thorough bookkeeper who holds on to representative student products for sound evaluation.

The Importance of a Mentor

One of the most invigorating and crucial activities for a beginner writing a portfolio is the collaborative effort between the instructor and a mentor who helps steer the direction of the document to meet the needs of improvement or assessment. Virtually all literature on portfolios urges faculty to enlist the creative, supportive help of a mentor. In the bulletin *Teaching Excellence*, for example, Seldin and Annis (1991–92) argue that a portfolio "is best prepared in consultation with others," suggesting that a trained mentor flushes out objective information that is evident or readily discovered in a teacher's work. The mentor's primary role is to help a colleague improve instruction in actual ways with definite products of good teaching, just the kind of supportive scrutiny a beginning teacher needs.

In some institutions, formal use of portfolios and existing mentoring programs for beginning teachers are often complementary. For example, at Columbia College of South Carolina, where fully a third or more of undergraduate students are in teacher certification tracks in their respective disciplines, the Department of English, rather than the Department of Education, has taken the lead in introducing student teachers to portfolios, helping young trainees in English to ponder values, methods, and goals and to work deliberately in their practicums to begin gathering hard information about their teaching. The English student teachers' enhanced skills of critical thinking and cogent writing combine with the careful, close mentoring of their advisor in the major to enable the department's chief advocate of portfolios to work with the beginners in writing vitally useful portfolios that obviously give them a vast head start in shaping a career predicated on taking teaching seriously and on valuing continual improvement. Naturally, such beginners also have an edge in finding jobs, for they have clearly demonstrated thoughtfulness about teaching, commitment to enhanced performance and to solid documentation of achievement, and confidence as reflective practitioners.

The Future of Portfolios

As American education continues to reform and to explore more effective and thorough assessment of faculty, the portfolio emerges as a crucial facet in the process of revaluing teaching. Undergraduate trainees and entry-level instructors benefit from the portfolio's efficacious design to make teaching a more self-conscious craft. The portfolio is not the only means of describing and documenting teaching effort, but it is the only instrument that concurrently improves instruction through the process of reflective writing and evaluates performance within a framework of narration and evidence.

In taking a concentrated three or four days to write a creditable portfolio with the crucial assistance of a mentor, a new teacher feels empowered to think about teaching, an obvious but vital component of improvement for beginners. The portfolio's process of written reflection invokes the power of narration, the ability of writing to make the often-unrecognized dimensions of teaching visible and understood by a community of readers. As a consequence of the mentoring process, the instructor also learns the value of collaboration in defining responsibilities, discussing values and methods, providing important supportive information, and delineating goals. Finally, the beginning teacher becomes more intentional in generating actual products of good teaching, making students the real beneficiaries of the work that goes into a portfolio.

References

Edgerton, Russell, Patricia Hutchings, and Kathleen Quinlan. 1991. *The Teaching Portfolio: Capturing the Scholarship in Teaching.* Washington, DC: American Association for Higher Education.

O'Neil, M. Carol, and W. Alan Wright. 1991. *Recording Teaching Accomplishment: A Dalhousie Guide to the Teaching Dossier.* Halifax, N.S.: Office of Instructional Development and Technology, Dalhousie University.

Seldin, Peter. 1991. *The Teaching Portfolio: A Practical Guide to Improved Performance and Promotion/Tenure Decisions.* Bolton, MA: Anker.

Seldin, Peter, and Linda F. Annis. 1991–92. "The Teaching Portfolio." *Teaching Excellence: Toward the Best in the Academy* 3.2: Professional and Organizational Development Network in Higher Education.

Seldin, Peter, and Associates. 1993. *Successful Use of Teaching Portfolios.* Bolton, MA: Anker.

Shore, B. M., et al. 1986. *The Teaching Dossier: A Guide to Its Preparation and Use.* Rev. ed. Montreal: Canadian Association of University Teachers.

Urbach, Floyd. 1992. "Developing a Teaching Portfolio." *College Teaching* 40: 71–74.

Editor

Ira Hayes is in his thirty-fifth year of teaching; he has spent the last fourteen years as supervisor of English at Syosset High School on Long Island. He has been a member-at-large of CEL and served on its program committee. He is currently on NCTE's Advisory Committee to Recognize Excellence in Student Literary Magazines. He has served in positions of leadership on New York State, New York City, and Long Island English education organizations. His other educational interest is Latin American culture and the Spanish language.

Contributors

Charlotte Adomaitis is currently assistant principal and supervisor of English at Thomas Jefferson High School, Brooklyn, New York. She has been an educator for twenty-one years, the past fifteen with the Board of Education of the City of New York. She serves on the Board of Directors of NCTE; is active in her state affiliate, NYSEC; and serves on the Board of Directors of her local affiliate, ELAC.

Janet Gebhart Auten is on the faculty at American University in Washington, D.C., where she teaches composition and women's/gender studies courses. Her published research includes articles on teacher commentary, student reading, and antebellum American writing. Her recent research focuses on the different evaluative languages that teachers and students bring to reading student writing.

Lisa Birnbaum is associate professor of English at the University of Tampa, where she teaches writing and literature and directs the Saunders Writing Center. She recently completed a two-year appointment as director of the university's first-year writing and writing-across-the-curriculum programs. As liaison for English and education, she has taught methods courses and supervised interns in middle and high school English classrooms. She has authored or co-authored a number of articles on the teaching of writing, the development of writing abilities, and writing center theory and practice.

Judith A. Boccia is assistant professor of education and director of the Center for Field Services and Studies at the University of Massachusetts–Lowell. She coordinates school-college collaborative projects for the university and also teaches in the graduate program in teaching. In addition to extensive study of beginning teacher concerns, presented at several national conferences, her recent research and publications focus on longitudinal studies of school-university partnerships.

Noreen Duffy Copeland is currently principal of Holy Ghost Catholic School in Albuquerque, New Mexico. She continues to meet with a teacher support group. The goal of this group is to encourage professional development while supporting teaching and learning. In addition, she trains faculty members and students in dispute-resolution skills for the Mediation in the Schools program.

Brenda L. Dyer has taught English as a second/foreign language in Canada, Portugal, and Japan. In Tokyo, she has taught English composition, literature, and women's studies to Japanese students of Temple University, International Christian University, and Chuo University. She is also the author-editor of an ESL anthology of North American literature, *Power Play*. She currently teaches English at Tokyo Woman's University.

Julia M. Emig co-founded the Bridge School in Chelsea, Massachusetts, in 1994. The Bridge is a public school within Chelsea High that engages students through integrated curriculum, projects and internships, and strong connections between faculty and students. Every Bridge School course incorporates off-site field experiences and labs as well as classroom visits from practitioners and experts in the fields of mathematics, science, humanities, community planning, etc.

Susan Joan Fishbein taught English at Westbury High School for nineteen years, chairing the English department for the last six of those years. She became assistant principal at East Meadow High School, East Meadow, New York, in 1993, where her responsibilities include being administrative liaison to the English Department. She is currently pursuing a doctoral degree in educational administration at Hofstra University.

Regina Paxton Foehr, Chair of the NCTE Assembly for Expanded Perspectives on Learning, teaches writing and English methods courses at Illinois State University. As reflected in her recent co-edited book, *The Spiritual Side of Writing: Releasing the Learner's Whole Potential,* Boynton/Cook, her research interests include the role of the unconscious and other forces that affect how we write, think, and learn.

Richard F. Gaspar is currently on the faculty at Van Buren Middle School in Tampa, Florida, where he is the English department chair and serves in numerous other positions. He earned his Ph.D. from the University of South Florida in 1997. During the 1997–1998 school year, he received the "Hillsborough County Schools Teacher of the Year" and "Florida Secondary Reading Teacher of the Year" awards. He has published in NCTE's *Ideas Plus,* the *Florida English Journal,* the *New Mexico Journal of Reading,* the *Journal of Interactive Instruction and Development,* and *Learning.* He is an active member of the National Council of Teachers of English, as well as other educational organizations, and is an active presenter at local, state, and national conferences.

F. Todd Goodson taught English in secondary schools in Missouri and Kansas for nine years. Currently, he is assistant professor of English at East Carolina University, where he teaches courses in pedagogy and serves as co-director of the Coastal Plains Writing Project. He is also co-editor of *The Writers' Slate,* a national journal of student writing (K–12).

Jane E. Harvey teaches at Brattleboro Union High School in Brattleboro, Vermont, where she advises the literary magazine and co-advises the senior class. She was a three-year recipient of a Dewitt Wallace Readers Digest Foundation Fellowship at the Bread Loaf School of English where she is pursuing an M.A. She is also a 1991 fellow of the Connecticut Writing Project and a published poet. She has recently completed an M.Ed. at the University of Connecticut.

Paul Heilker teaches courses in the theory of rhetoric, writing, and composition pedagogy at Virginia Tech, where he serves as the Director of the First-Year Writing Programs. His work has appeared in such journals as *Rhetoric Review, Computers and Composition,* and *Composition Studies.* He is the author of *The Essay: Theory and Practice for an Active Form* (NCTE, 1996) and co-editor of *Keywords in Composition Studies* (Boynton/Cook, 1996).

Daniel A. Heller is Director of Professional Development at Brattleboro Union High School in Vermont. He has published articles on supervision, teacher empowerment, and school community partnerships for the Association for Supervision and Curriculum Development, Phi Delta Kappa, and NCTE's *English Journal.* He recently completed two years as editor of "This World of English" in *English Journal.* His areas of professional focus include professional development and alternative learning programs for nontraditional students.

Mary Theresa Kyne currently serves as chair of the Department of English and assistant professor at Seton Hill College in Greensburg, Pennsylvania. She serves on the Advisory Board of the Western Pennsylvania Symposium on World Literatures (WPSWL), where she also serves as secretary to the director and assistant editor of the *Selected Proceedings.* Her publications include the book *Country Parsons, Country Poets.*

Gerald Mackey is the Palmer Campus director and professor of English at Trident Technical College in Charleston, South Carolina. He is a former high school teacher and coordinator of teacher evaluation. A member of NCTE and other educational organizations, he has won numerous awards throughout his professional career and published widely in a number of professional journals.

Diana Wagner Marmaluk received her B.A. in English from Alverno College in Milwaukee and her M.A. from Beaver College in Glenside, Pennsylvania. She currently teaches freshman writing and coordinates campus tutoring services at Beaver College.

Jennifer S. McConnell currently serves as the Adult Services Coordinator for the Technical Center at Springfield (Vermont). She is working on her master's degree in administration and supervision at Antioch New England. In addition to her duties at the Technical Center, she serves on a variety of committees in her school district, and she organizes the district-wide orientation program for new teachers.

Mary C. McMackin is assistant professor in the School of Education at Lesley College, Cambridge, Massachusetts. She is also a consultant in the Somerville Public Schools, where she provides staff development workshops and monitors an innovative intervention program for at-risk first-grade readers. She has had articles published in *Childhood Education* and the *Clearing House.* In addition, she presents regularly at local, regional, and national conferences.

Sean Meehan taught eighth- and tenth-grade English for three years at Newark Academy in Livingston, New Jersey. Most recently he has divided his time between work on an autobiography in progress, entitled *Prologue,* and graduate studies. Currently, he is in the doctoral program in English at the University of Iowa.

Maureen Neal is currently teaching composition, literature, and English education courses at Mesa State College in Grand Junction, Colorado. She has written articles and conference papers on portfolio grading, social constructionism and expressionism, academic register, and hyperfluency and is currently at work on a manuscript which explores the nature and function of classroom talk in academic settings.

Thomas Philion is assistant professor in the Department of English at the University of Illinois at Chicago, and assistant director of the Secondary English Teacher Education program. His publications consist of articles in *English Journal, Illinois English Bulletin,* and the NCTE collection *Focus on Reflecting and Connecting.* A former middle school teacher, he is involved in collaborative research projects with urban educators involving computers, collaborative learning, and reading pedagogy.

Gayle Bolt Price is chair of the English Department, director of the Writing Center, and professor of English at Gardner-Webb University in Boiling Springs, North Carolina. Her publications include articles in *Research in the Teaching of English, College Composition and Communication, Phi Delta Kappan,* and *Not for Children Only: Great Books for All Ages.* A former high school teacher and director of learning assistance programs, she teaches composition, young adult literature, and English education courses, and supervises student teachers in English.

Sheryl Rubin is chairperson of the English Department at Oceanside High School in Oceanside, New York, and adjunct instructor of methods of teaching English in the School of Education at Long Island University, C. W. Post Campus. She is president of the Long Island Language Arts Council.

Donald M. Shafer is English Department chair at Fairview High School in Fairview Park, Ohio. He has given numerous presentations at NTCE conventions and conferences and is currently Secretary of the Conference on English Leadership. His publications include contributions on government policy and classroom pedagogy.

Kenneth Simons teaches English at Syosset High School in Syosset, New York. He received his Ph.D. in English and Comparative Literature from Columbia University in 1980. His publications include *The Ludic Imagination: A Reading of Joseph Conrad* and an essay on Conrad's "Youth" in *Marlow,* edited by Harold Bloom.

Inga Harmon Smith is currently engaged in doing staff development for English/language arts teachers, grades 6–12. Her time is divided between serving as a National Language Arts Consultant for McDougel Littell Publisher and as a freelance consultant for her own company, Communications Unlimited.

Susan A. Wasserman, Professor Emeritus, is director of the California funded Beginning Teacher Support and Assessment Program at California State University–Northridge. An educator for over thirty years, she has maintained an active publications and presentation career and has specialized in teacher preparation, in addition to other areas of research and teaching.

Debra J. Williams holds a B.A. from the University of Vermont and an M.A. from the Bread Loaf School of English at Middlebury College. She has taught English at Brattleboro Union High School, Brattleboro, Vermont, for four years. She has also taught in New Hampshire and Colorado, and has served as high school drama director, class advisor, and speech coach.

Wang Zhijun was a middle school English teacher for eight years and for the past decade has been a faculty member at Huazhong University of Science and Engineering in the People's Republic of China. Her publications include the *College English Usage Dictionary*. She has won numerous awards for her teaching.

John Zubizarreta is professor of English and director of Honors at Columbia College of South Carolina. Selected as the 1994–95 Carnegie Foundation/CASE Professor for South Carolina, he has also earned recognition for teaching and scholarly excellence from a number of national and regional organizations. He has published regularly on American and comparative literatures, teaching improvement, and teaching portfolios.

This book was typeset in Palatino and Helvetica by
City Desktop Productions, Inc.
The typefaces used on the cover were Palatino, Slimbach, and Benguiat Gothic.
The book was printed on 50-lb. Smooth Offset by V. G. Reed and Sons, Inc.